System Support for
Security and Privacy in Pervasive Computing

Dissertation

zur Erlangung des akademischen Grades eines

Doktors der Naturwissenschaften
(Dr. rer. nat.)

durch die Fakultät für Wirtschaftswissenschaftlichen der

Universität Duisburg-Essen
Campus Essen

vorgelegt von

Wolfgang Apolinarski

aus Leverkusen

Essen, 2015

Erstgutachter: Prof. Dr. rer. nat. habil. Pedro José Marrón,
                   Universität Duisburg-Essen
Zweitgutachter: Prof. Dr. rer. nat. Gregor Schiele,
                   Universität Duisburg-Essen

Tag der mündlichen Prüfung: 21.04.2016

Bibliografische Information der Deutschen Nationalbibliothek

Die Deutsche Nationalbibliothek verzeichnet diese Publikation in der
Deutschen Nationalbibliografie; detaillierte bibliografische Daten sind
im Internet über http://dnb.d-nb.de abrufbar.

ISBN 978-3-8325-4269-6

Logos Verlag Berlin GmbH
Comeniushof, Gubener Str. 47,
10243 Berlin
Tel.: +49 (0)30 42 85 10 90
Fax: +49 (0)30 42 85 10 92
INTERNET: http://www.logos-verlag.de

Contents

Contents

List of Figures

List of Tables

Abstract

One of the main goals of the pervasive computing domain is to provide the user with task support for everyday tasks. This task support should be realized by pervasive applications that are seamlessly integrated in the environment, for example into embedded, resource-constrained devices such as everyday objects. The interaction with the pervasive applications should be minimized for the user, they should not be distracted by them. In the end, the fact that pervasive technology is involved, should disappear from the perception of the user. This requires the pervasive applications to be deeply integrated into the current environment of a user. Often, system support is required to help to develop pervasive applications. Additionally, it provides developers with an already integrated environment that can share common knowledge of the situation of a user with applications they develop.

The situation of a user is usually expressed by context information that may contain private information which should not be accessible to the public. System support should therefore contain mechanisms that utilize security and privacy methods when handling context. Pervasive applications can then use these mechanisms and create pervasive environments while preserving the user's privacy.

This work's contribution is the development of security and privacy mechanisms in pervasive middlewares. First, we show how context information can be processed and queried in a privacy-preserving manner. By securing the authenticity and integrity of context information and creating a secure context distribution algorithm, we show how pervasive applications can use and share context securely. Second, we introduce secure role assignment as a mechanism for environment adaptation which is built on context information. Similarly to context, roles need to be protected and secured during distribution. Additionally, we add system support for secure roles which can be used for role-based access control by pervasive applications. Third, we create a secure key-exchange mechanism that can be used to secure the communication between users and devices. This is an essential step that needs to be performed before any private information can be shared among them. Fourth, we introduce a framework for the automatic generation of a privacy policy. This framework creates an individual privacy policy that can be used to share context between users, devices or applications while preserving the user's will with regard to context privacy.

All these mechanisms are integrated into a pervasive middleware that provides system support for pervasive applications. We have shown the feasibility of our work by the creation of several pervasive applications that make use of our four contributions. The applications were developed during the European research projects *PECES* and *GAMBAS*. In PECES, the first two approaches contribute to a pervasive middleware that allows the secure formation of a pervasive environment called *smart space*, including hierarchical grouping and secure communication among devices. Often, several pervasive environments exist next to each other as so-called islands of integration. Here, each island consists of a fully functioning pervasive environment, but does not support the interaction with other islands. Using hierarchical grouping, the PECES middleware allows them to overcome the islands of integration. In GAMBAS, the pervasive middleware was extended with the second two approaches that allow a secure user-level authentication and therefore the sharing of context information in a privacy-preserving way. For this, a mechanism was designed that uses online collaboration tools such as Facebook or Google Calendar to piggyback a key-exchange on them. In the project, several context detection mechanisms were developed and integrated which makes the GAMBAS middleware an ideal platform for a wide range of pervasive applications.

In this dissertation, all contributions are described and discussed in detail. Several pervasive applications are presented that benefit from the system support which was created by these contributions. In the end, a thorough evaluation shows the applicability of them to the pervasive computing domain and its resource-constrained, embedded devices while providing a high level of security and privacy to the user.

1 Introduction

In this chapter, we introduce the topic of this thesis. At first, we will start with a motivation that discusses the vision of pervasive computing and the challenges that we are facing. Then, we will describe our contribution to the area of security and privacy in this domain. Finally, we will present the structure of the main parts of this thesis.

1.1 Motivation

One of the main goals of applications that are executed in the pervasive computing domain is to create environments that provide users with seamless and distraction-free task support. Often, the task support is realized by so-called pervasive applications that are running on devices integrated into everyday objects. The set of everyday objects is not limited to devices that are already regarded as *smart* such as smart phones, but also include devices like refrigerators, coffee machines, light controls, power switches and other devices from everyday life. Furthermore, smart street lamps, smart ticketing and payment systems, smart homes and smart cars are already extending the size of such environments or *smart spaces* from small, local and isolated solutions to a ubiquitous, worldwide intelligent smart space that itself consists of several interacting smart spaces.

During the realization of this vision, we face several challenges. The configuration of one smart device might already be cumbersome, but the combination of several devices into a smart space usually requires knowledge of communication protocols that is not available to the average user. Similarly, the combination of several smart spaces to one overarching smart space is even more challenging for average users. One of the solutions (and a challenge itself) to this is the acquisition of context information through sensors that are often built into these smart devices. Additionally, the devices usually feature actuators that need to be configured such that they can be used in smart spaces to manipulate the physical world. Since the devices are highly integrated, they are also heterogeneous with regard to many aspects such as processor type, RAM size and power consumption. If we now consider additional factors such as mobility, it becomes clear that we are dealing with a highly dynamic environment. The automatic configuration of such a smart space and the introduction of common communication protocols or middlewares are therefore further challenges. Since it needs permanent adaptation to be able to cope with such dynamic smart spaces, manual adaptation by the user is not distraction-free nor feasible. As a consequence, another important challenge is the development of an automated adaptation usually also performed by a middleware.

The security aspects of these challenges are often disregarded, since the first priority is usually to provide a working (technical) solution to each challenge. Nowadays, there already exist several approaches that solve (parts of) the problems of smart spaces in the pervasive computing domain. Often, these approaches were created without security in mind and are thus inherently insecure. Of course, solving the technical challenges is important for the further development of interacting devices in smart spaces, but now, we are at a stage where we need to introduce security, either by adapting the existing technical solutions or by re-designing them. Establishing security in the pervasive computing domain, for example by introducing secure smart spaces or intelligent environments, is a complex challenge. To ensure a secure smart space, all parts of the smart space must be secured. This includes, but is not limited to, the physical devices, all steps of the smart space formation, which is usually based on context information, device interactions and other configuration adaptations.

Security and especially secure communication are usually a requirement, i.e, an important aspect of automatically configured intelligent environments and are usually a requirement for privacy. Imagine an adaptation decision that results in displaying a secret document on a public screen set up by a malicious user. The screen could easily be programmed to copy the document against the intents of the document authors. Similarly, while this would only result in intellectual property being stolen (or result in a breach of privacy), devices like doors or smart cars without a proper security implementation will result in the theft of real goods. To overcome these issues, it is necessary, as a first step, to secure the primitives that form the basis for adaptation decisions, namely the context information.

The work that is presented in this thesis is therefore a first step to establish secure and privacy-aware mechanisms for the pervasive computing domain by creating secure smart spaces or intelligent environments. We concentrate particularly on the context-dependent formation process of smart spaces and the exchange of context or data between devices in such environments. We present here four security and privacy mechanisms. The first two concentrate on how automated adaptation decisions can be secured to establish secure smart spaces or intelligent environments. The next two concentrate on the secure exchange of data between devices in these environments. Here, the focus lies on the secure and privacy-preserving interaction of devices and/or pervasive applications.

1.2 Contribution

This thesis and the work it is based on contributes to the field of pervasive/ubiquitous computing. In particular, it contributes to the area of security and privacy in the pervasive computing domain and is focused on a) the development of secure middlewares and b) on secure interactions in smart spaces or intelligent environments.

In this thesis, we discuss different concepts for the introduction of security and privacy in the pervasive computing domain. Although there already exist many pervasive applications, security and privacy is often disregarded and only discussed as *future work*. With our work, we want to change this and show that it is feasible to create secure and privacy-aware pervasive applications. We hope that our work leads to a change in the development of pervasive applications by showing that designing them securely and in a privacy-preserving way is possible and can be carried out with only little overhead in application development and execution.

We start with two security and privacy mechanisms that improve the state of the art by introducing security in the formation of smart spaces. Additionally, the resulting environment configuration allows to perform role-based access control securely. The two other mechanisms describe how a peer-based data exchange in pervasive applications can be secured properly by executing a key exchange and deriving a privacy policy automatically that, in the end, preserves a user's privacy.

The first two approaches for peer-based context management that we introduce in Chapter 4, show how adequate support for context acquisition and management in a peer-based environment like the pervasive computing domain can be provided. Here, we focus on creating middleware support for these tasks. Since the context management is peer-based, it is by design preserving privacy, because the data is not stored on and cannot be retrieved from a third-party server, but is only stored on the users' own devices. Supporting the secure context distribution, we additionally present a secure, distributed and also peer-based verification system for context information. It allows decentralized context distribution that is not dependent on any kind of infrastructure. Additionally, sensors can sense context independently and issue a context token that can later be validated. The mechanisms for peer-based context management that are described in this chapter can be used to secure context which forms the basis for the formation of smart spaces or intelligent environments.

The second approach for introducing security and privacy in the pervasive computing domain is describing how roles can be used as the next logical step in the formation process of smart spaces. Roles are essentially tags based on context information and are used for the configuration and adaptation of environments used by pervasive applications in the pervasive computing domain. The assignment of roles allows to form smart spaces or intelligent environments in a flexible, application-overarching manner. While the idea of role assignment itself is not new, the introduction and implementation of security mechanisms show how security and privacy can be established in the formation process of smart spaces. Additionally, we show how the interaction in a smart space can be secured when secure roles are distributed. The usage of secure roles in smart spaces also allows the execution of secure role-based access control. This enables the use of role-based access control in security critical pervasive scenarios.

When performing secure interactions in smart spaces, it can – depending on the scenario – be required to know that the communication partner is authenticated and that the communication channel is encrypted. In the pervasive computing domain, there exist several approaches to secure the communication channel. Most of them are based on key-exchanges that need to be performed by the communication partners. One of the most commonly used models – also used across the Internet – is the utilization of certificate hierarchies that can secure key-exchanges through digital signatures. This model is usually suitable for client-server interactions and cannot be easily adopted for user-to-user communication. In contrast to that, our approach *PIKE* is based on the use of online collaboration tools such as Google Calendar or Facebook that have become a ubiquitous mediator of human interactions. Our key-exchange protocols PIKE and P2PIKE show how the configuration effort for secure communication can be minimized by using these tools. Again, PIKE and P2PIKE are suitable for secure peer-to-peer group and client-server interactions, making them a universal tool which can be used by applications build for the pervasive computing domain.

Our final contribution to the field of security and privacy in the pervasive computing domain is the automated privacy policy generation. Many pervasive computing applications share context between users or devices. In the past, a significant amount of research has been focusing on the aspect of effective and efficient context recognition. Yet, when context is shared with others, the resulting disclosure of personal information can have undesirable privacy implications. For example, context information may contain private information (like the location) that should not be shared with every user, but only with close relatives. A common solution to this problem is the manual creation of an application-specific privacy policy that defines which information should be shared with whom. While it may be possible for a user to define a privacy policy for one pervasive application, the efforts increase with the number of pervasive applications which each may use its own privacy language. Our work on automating the privacy policy generation therefore uses online collaboration tools such as Facebook to analyze the user's sharing behavior. In the end, the framework that we developed allows us to automatically create a privacy policy that – by the use of our pervasive middleware – can be shared among pervasive applications.

All major contributions described in this thesis have been published at international scientific conferences, namely PERWARE 2010 [AHM10], CONTEXT 2011 [AHPM11], IE 2011 [AHM11], IE 2012 [AHM12], PERCOM 2013 [AHIM13b] and IE 2015 [AHM15]. An extended version of the fifth paper is also published in the PMC journal [AHIM14] and an extended version of the last paper has been invited for a journal publication. The paper presented at IE 2012 in Mexico [AHM12] has won the best full paper award. Papers or demo papers that extend the work presented here were also presented at PERCOM 2013 [AHIM13a] (demo paper) and PerCity 2014 [AIP14]. Additionally, a keynote at the WoRIE 2015 workshop [Apo15] was held that described our first three contributions. The results of the research presented here were applied in two European projects. The middleware of both the PECES (PErvasive Computing in Embedded Systems) project [PEC10] and the GAMBAS (Generic Adaptive Middleware for Behaviour-driven Autonomous Services) [GAM12] project integrates the results presented here. Some findings were also implemented in the NARF (NARF Activity Recognition Framework) [HIA+10] project.

1.3 Structure

The remaining parts of the thesis are structured as follows. In the following chapter, we discuss the field of pervasive computing and in detail the security and privacy challenges. Additionally, we describe the middleware and pervasive applications that integrate the privacy and security mechanisms discussed in this thesis. The prototypical applications were developed within the European projects PECES and GAMBAS. We therefore briefly outline the scope of these projects. This provides an overview over the topics that are then discussed in the remaining parts of this thesis in detail.

In Chapter 3, we discuss related work and identify gaps. There, we derive general requirements that build the ground for the following Chapters 4 to 7 which discuss our approaches for security and privacy in the pervasive computing domain. Chapter 4 is focused on the security of context and describes the peer-based context management and secure context distribution framework. In Chapter 5, we describe how role assignment can be performed securely. Thereafter, our key-exchange protocol PIKE is presented in Chapter 6. It shows how a key-exchange can be performed between users using online collaboration tools. Our last contribution is described in Chapter 7, where we show a framework that automates the generation of a privacy policy, also by using online collaboration tools. All four contributions to the field of security and privacy in the pervasive computing domain are discussed thoroughly.

A detailed evaluation of our work is presented in Chapter 8 and refers to our contributions and the derived requirements. Finally, Chapter 9 concludes the thesis and our contributions to the field of security and privacy that were presented in the previous chapters. Additionally, we discuss possible extensions to our work and give a brief and more general overview of work that could be carried out in the future.

2 Pervasive Computing Concepts

In this chapter, we introduce several concepts that will be discussed in this thesis. At first, we discuss the concept of *pervasive computing* with a special focus on primitives like context and roles and software design ideas for pervasive middlewares. At the end, we briefly discuss the role of devices in the pervasive computing domain. A separate section is then presenting the common security goals. We focus on the security goals that are realized in the work described in this thesis.

The last section presents different prototypical applications that were implemented in European projects. The technology presented in this thesis has been developed and was applied in these projects. While the security-relevant parts of the applications are described in a greater detail in Section 4 to 7, we present here an overview of the projects and the prototypical applications, such that the reader receives a complete view.

2.1 Pervasive Computing

The domain of pervasive computing was first described in detail by Mark Weiser [Wei91] who coined the term *Ubiquitous Computing*. Ubiquitous or pervasive computing describe a vision where computers are part of the environment and are not recognized by users as actual computers, but as a normal part of their everyday life. In his vision, Weiser described interacting devices of different sizes, ubiquitous applications that were "peregrinating" between devices and showed first hardware prototypes. He acknowledged privacy as a key for the realization of ubiquitous computing.

The idea of pervasive computing is to provide users support for everyday user tasks. Additionally, this support should be *distraction-free* for the user and the computers that realize the support should be integrated *seamlessly* in the environment. Distraction-free in the context of pervasive computing means that users can intuitively use pervasive applications for their tasks without having to interact with the application or even without having to configure it first. This usually requires a high amount of automation from the side of the pervasive application. The user should not be distracted of his or her original tasks by the support the application provides. The term seamless is often described as a stage of integration that actually makes the technology/computer that the user is using disappear. While using a pervasive application, the user might not even notice that he or she is using a computer. Often, this is realized by using small, embedded devices and/or highly intuitive user interfaces.

Nowadays, there have been several attempts and ideas for the realization of the vision of pervasive computing, especially with a focus on automating the environment configuration. Usually, these approaches use context information gathered by sensors that are deployed in the environment or built-in (e.g., in smartphones). This context is then used to distribute or assign roles which describe what function each of the devices in the pervasive environment should fulfill. Often, a middleware is used for the interactions between the devices (bridging different communication technologies), but also for storing/retrieving context and the assignment of roles. These middlewares must be able to run on many types of (embedded) devices that are used in a pervasive computing environment. We provide here a brief overview on the topics *context*, *roles*, *middlewares* and *devices*. The focus of this description lies in a short, general view on each topic that provides the basis for the security-centric view that we adopt for the remaining parts of the thesis.

2.1.1 Context

In the pervasive computing domain, context is usually used to support the automatic environment configuration. There exist several definitions of the term *context*. We used the definition from Becker [Bec04], which is based on the definition of Dey et al. [DA99]. It states:

"Context is the information which can be used to characterize the situation of an entity. Entities are persons, locations, or objects which are considered to be relevant for the behavior of an application. The entity itself is regarded as part of its context." [Bec04]

For the automation of pervasive environment configuration, the situation of an entity, i.e., any relevant object for the behavior of an application, is crucial. When the situation is known, the application can be configured fully automated, in the majority of cases. It is noteworthy that the user herself is also a relevant object. Imagine a smart home environment that starts the coffee machine in the morning. Of course, the state of the user (awake or sleeping) is a relevant information for the environment that decides on the time the brewing process is started.

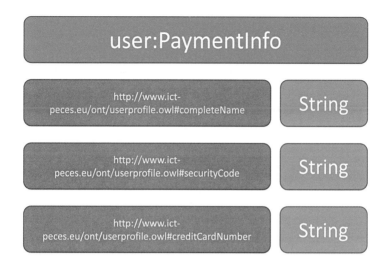

Figure 2.1: Three Context Triples from PECES [PEC10]

Additionally, the definition from Becker is not only constrained to entities that interact with the applications, but also includes objects that are not relevant to the actual interaction, but may change (i.e., are relevant for) the behavior of a pervasive application. An example for this may be the surrounding noise during interactions with the application, this could be seen as context (*noise level*) and the application may adapt its configuration by increasing or decreasing the volume of attached speakers.

Similarly, other context information are relevant to the configuration of pervasive applications and a change in context often triggers a configuration adaption for pervasive applications. Only the constant adaptation reduces the manual configuration steps that the user has to perform and can therefore be regarded as *distraction-free* (to the user).

The representation of context information used in this thesis is using the RDF language [Wora]. As can be seen in Figure 2.1, this is a rather complex language that uses subject, predicate, object (SPO) syntax. The figure displays three triples with the subject *user:PaymentInfo* that is colored in blue. The predicates are each displayed in orange and denote the (context) type of the information, such as the complete name of a user. The object itself is only displayed by its type variable (in green). In this example, the object must be a text string. Together, these three triples form the context

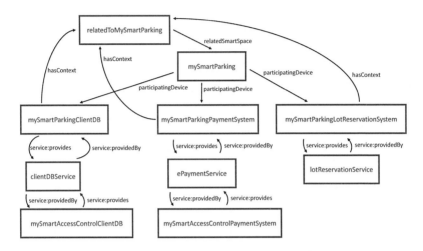

Figure 2.2: A Context Ontology from PECES [PEC10]

information *payment info* from a user that is identified by his complete name (in this example). In general, it is also possible to link triples together (similarly to reference another dataset in conventional data bases).

Any meta information, like the relationship of different context to each other is stored in a so-called ontology. An example ontology from the PECES project [PEC10] is displayed in Figure 2.2. A modeled ontology is usually one of the first steps to create an overview of the pervasive computing scenario for which an application should be developed.

Besides the format of the context information, also the detection of context is an important factor for the development of pervasive applications. Usually, parts of the context (like the device's owner) of an entity may be known in advance and can be configured by the user or during an installation routine. Also, mobile devices that join and leave pervasive environments may be detected easily by means of communication protocols and range (Bluetooth, WiFi). Other context information that may be relevant for configuration adaptations (e.g., a user's location or moving speed) must be detected by other means.

Often, sensors that are deployed in the environment may detect additional context information and make them available through a middleware or other means of pervasive infrastructure. In general, these sensors are not necessary trustworthy, especially when they are run by a third party. Since we are focusing on peer-to-peer networking pervasive computing applications, we often use the built-in context detection abilities of the devices (e.g., smartphones) themselves.

As will be further discussed in Section 2.1.4, smartphones are an important development platform for pervasive applications. Smartphones have a number of built-in sensors that can be used directly for context detection. The types of sensors that may be included (depending on the model) are accelerometers, a digital compass, GPS receivers, proximity sensor, light sensor, etc. These sensors provide measurements that can be combined with sensor-like features such as a camera, microphone or NFC. In the end, it is possible to detect context directly on a smartphone. An example toolkit is the NARF Activity Recognition Framework [HIA+10] that can be used for context detection on pervasive devices. The detected context can then be used to adapt the configuration of a pervasive environment.

2.1.2 Roles

Essentially, a role is a tag that is assigned to a device by a role assignment service. This tag is usually associated with a functionality that can be exploited by a pervasive application. Often, the role assignment process was also triggered by the pervasive application to perform an application configuration. An example could be a text editor pervasive application that is running on a smartphone, but also supports bigger screens and input devices like keyboards. It will scan the environment for these device types and will then migrate the application window to these devices, if applicable.

In the work that we are presenting in this thesis, roles are assigned on the basis of rules that evaluate context information, e.g., filter on context. Roles are therefore the next abstraction level, based on context. Similarly to the context detection services, the role assignment process of a pervasive environment is constantly running and checking for context changes that may trigger changes in the role distribution. An example of this can be seen in Figure 2.3 and 2.4 that show a smart home with its context and the resulting role assignment after the evaluation of the role specification by a role assignment service.

The responsible role assignment device is – in this case – a smart home server. In general, this role is fulfilled by a static device with the lowest constrains on resources. The main reason for this is the overhead for the management of roles and the filtering of context that requires additional processing power. In a more mobile environment, the role of the role assigning device can be

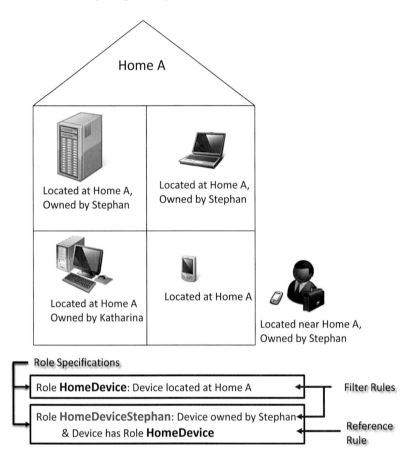

Figure 2.3: A Smart Home with Context and a Role Specification

handed over regularly, depending on context information like battery power, processing capabilities or round-robin.

In general, devices are not forced to take part in the role assignment process. A device can decide, if it takes part. This is important, since the role assignment process might require that context information of the participant is revealed at least to the role assigning device (possibly run by a third party). The decision can be taken by each device individually, for example by using a pre-configured list of trusted devices.

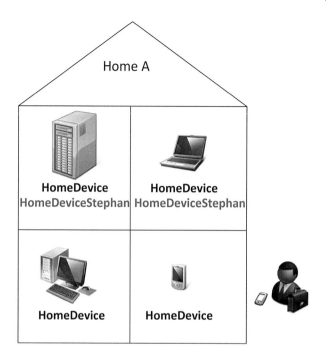

Figure 2.4: Roles Assigned to Devices in a Smart Home According to the Specification from Figure 2.3

The roles that are distributed by a role assignment service can also be used for role-based access control (RBAC). To allow a secure and authenticated use of roles in RBAC, the roles must be secured and the device a role is assigned to must also be authenticated. More details on the use of roles in RBAC is given in Chapter 5. An example use case of RBAC would be an administrator that carries his smartphone that is connected to his employer's infrastructure. Instead of a key to open the doors to his office and another key for the server rooms, he could use the role that is assigned to his device to authenticate at the doors that would then open automatically (after successful validation).

2.1.3 System-support for Pervasive Computing

In general, pervasive applications should be configured automatically. They should automatically discover compatible pervasive devices in the environment and connect to them, making use of them, if they provide any use to the application or the user. To transfer this scenario to the real world, a common architecture is needed that unifies at least discovery and communication protocols. This allows pervasive devices which support this architecture to find each other and to communicate with each other. Similarly, data format standards must be openly shared among devices and applications to minimize incompatibilities between different device or application manufacturers.

These requirements for building an integrated pervasive computing environment can be fulfilled in different ways. A common approach is a centric, infrastructure-based server that manages the pervasive environment and all its applications. Examples for this kind of pervasive architecture are GAIA [RHC⁺02] or Aura [GSS02]. Similar to a cloud-based solution, pervasive applications and devices are connected to a server in the environment. This centralized approach enables the pervasive computing vision by using an omniscient, omnipotent server that transfers data and moves applications depending on the infrastructure that is connected to this server. The server infrastructure can usually be extended with several plug-ins that manage users, perform access control to a shared file storage, etc. While this is a powerful solution, it requires all devices to be connected to one infrastructure server, which is usually (e.g., for privacy reasons) not the case.

An alternative approach is the use of a peer-based middleware like BASE [HBS03] or MundoCore [AKM07]. Here, each device is capable of executing (at least parts of) the middleware. The middleware provides the basic functionalities such as peer-to-peer communication or device discovery on every device. Additionally, the middleware may contain components that allow the distribution of context and/or roles, depending on the computing capabilities of the device it is deployed on. This approach allows to build a peer-based pervasive environment that does not include a central authority or server. Because of its inherent privacy (each device does not need to share any information with a central server), we have used this approach as a basis to create the work that is presented in this thesis.

The middleware BASE has been extended to perform the tasks that were carried out in the European projects PECES and GAMBAS. The Chapters 4 and 5 describe the changes that we performed with regard to security and privacy. The middleware BASE is a communication middleware that allows the spontaneous communication between different devices. BASE

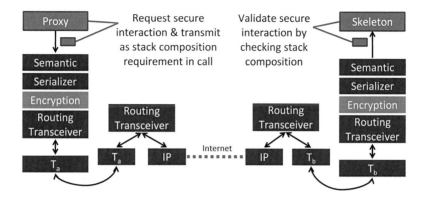

Figure 2.5: Communication Plug-ins for Secure Interaction in BASE

supports resource-constrained as well as powerful devices such as desktop PCs, servers, smartphones, routers and mobile phones. It is written in the Java programming language and can run even on older cell phones that support the J2ME (micro edition) Java profile.

BASE has a plug-in architecture that can be extended by application developers. One of the main functionality it provides is the communication across different communication technologies. This can be used by application developers directly, without the need to create own communication plug-ins. If necessary, any developer can also extended BASE by providing it with other communication protocols that add different communication technologies to BASE. Also, a simple service abstraction is included in BASE which has RMI/RPC functionality and can serialize Java objects.

Similarly, BASE's support for communication plug-ins allows to set up a communication stack that includes plug-ins for different semantics such as encrypted communication. Another advantage is that devices that route the packets do not need to decompose the complete packet, instead, they only use their routing transceiver to bridge communication technologies. An example can be seen in Figure 2.5 where the packet travels from the proxy to the skeleton by using three different technologies, T_a, IP and T_b.

In summary, the BASE middleware provides us with a complete toolkit for the development of pervasive applications. In this thesis, we extended BASE especially with regard to technologies that are useful for pervasive applications such as secure context distribution and role assignment. Besides

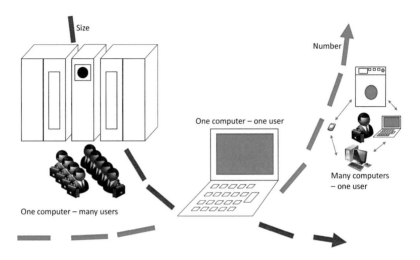

Figure 2.6: Computer Usage in the Course of Time

increasing the usefulness of BASE, this also shows how this pervasive middleware can be extended easily, providing system-support for the pervasive computing domain.

2.1.4 Devices

The original vision that Mark Weiser described was using tabs, pads and boards as the devices in the ubiquitous computing domain. Tabs were designed as small, integrated (i.e., embedded) devices that could be worn as a badge, but also include functions such as calendars, etc. Nowadays, tabs could be identified both with embedded devices like a sensor in a smart home (that has no user interface) and with smartphones. It is noteworthy that the original description separated them more by size than by function. Similarly, pads can be seen as tablet devices. Following the idea of Weiser, pads should not be carried around, but stay in a room, ready to be used by any user. Boards on the other hand cannot be carried, since they are big interactive displays that are installed on a wall. They can be compared with screens that have the necessary system software installed which makes them compatible with pervasive applications.

Also, the idea of Weiser that the usage of computers will change (as shown in Figure 2.6), has become true. In the beginning of the computer area, we were using one computer (mainframe) with many users. This changed with the appearance of the desktop PC where one computer had one user. With the emerging technologies, miniaturization, high wireless communication bandwidth and low power consumption, the vision has shifted. Now, we have one user that uses many computers and most of them are included into embedded devices (smartphones, MP3 players, smart watches) that are not easily recognizable for the user as a computer.

Of course, the idea of pervasive computing was refined during the development of devices and services. Almost every kind of device could now be integrated into a pervasive environment, from refrigerators and lamps over network devices like routers to computers with a user interface such as smartphones or desktop PCs. As described in the previous section, the software which provides system support must be executed on all these devices, i.e., support heterogeneous devices.

Besides the common criteria that concentrate on capabilities like CPU power, RAM size, battery size, etc., also the mobility of devices is an important factor that needs to be taken into account. While stationary devices like a refrigerator can be added permanently to a smart home environment, other devices such as smartphones, but also notebooks exhibit a mobility that must be taken into account when a pervasive scenario is designed. Also, it should be easy to add or remove devices to a pervasive environment, when devices with high mobility are considered by the scenario. The manifold devices that can be used in the pervasive computing domain is therefore adding complexity to the middleware. This must be taken into account during the design phase of pervasive applications or scenarios.

As described earlier in this work, we concentrate on peer-to-peer communication between devices. Nevertheless, resource-poor devices may have problems to manage all their context information, especially with regard to efficient querying the context to answer context requests. This is why we allow a resource-poor device to cooperate with a more powerful device, e.g., to manage its context. An example would be a home server that acts as a hub for battery-powered embedded devices. The opposite approach would be to have a server-based pervasive system such as the systems described in the previous section. In our work (and further outlined throughout this thesis), the peer-to-peer approach has been proven to be more flexible, scalable and privacy preserving. Nevertheless, we do not ban the use of a home server for a higher flexibility with regard to resource-poor devices.

2.2 Security Goals

The security goals describe different aspects of security. Often, the so-called *CIA* (confidentiality, integrity and availability) security goals are commonly regarded as important. In addition to these goals, also *authenticity* and *privacy* are important aspects that we considered during the creation of this work. There exist many other goals that are relevant for security, for example nonrepudiation or anonymity that are not or only partly considered in this thesis. The five security goals that we concentrated on, will be described shortly in the following.

2.2.1 Confidentiality

Often, communication channels should be protected from eavesdroppers, for example, when private data is transferred. But even data that is not regarded as private may leak information which may be useful for malicious devices or persons. Similarly, the pure fact that two or more devices are communicating with each other could give the attacker valuable information. Nevertheless, the first step is always to gain confidentiality for data. As a result, recent initiatives try to realize confidentiality for all kinds of communication data that is transfered over the Internet. Therefore, confidentiality should be considered during the design of systems for the pervasive computing domain, if possible.

The confidentiality security goal can be reached in different ways. One possible solution would be the creation of a dedicated communication channel that cannot be overheard easily, for example a direct ethernet cable between two devices in an access restricted area. While this might be a proper solution for infrastructure-based networks like they exist in a company, the pervasive computing domain features devices that exhibit a high mobility. Also, devices interact spontaneously with each other which requires a more flexible or wireless connection technology like Bluetooth or WiFi. The drawbacks of these technologies are that they often cannot provide confidentiality for the whole path the data is traveling.

Using an open communication channel, confidentiality can be supported by encryption. Many technologies like Bluetooth and WiFi can be configured to create encrypted communication channels that are then used for group communication. But often, these channels are not providing adequate confidentiality since the communication keys are widely known (e.g., may be printed and handed out to visitors). Also, communication in the pervasive computing domain should be agnostic with regard to communication technologies to provide a real end-to-end encryption. The use of a communication middleware allows to bridge these technologies and tries to abstract from them. In the end, concerning the pervasive computing domain, confidentiality should be provided by the middleware, usually through the means of encryption and not be technology dependent.

2.2.2 Integrity

While the security goal confidentiality keeps data private, the security goal integrity keeps the data unmodified. This security goal is orthogonal to confidentiality, because even data that can be overheard by third parties can be protected in such a way that it is not possible to alter it, i.e., keeping the integrity of the data. During the development of applications for the pervasive computing domain, data integrity is an important security goal since machine to machine communication is very error prone when it comes to data manipulation. Often, manipulated data may introduce a breach in security. In contrast to cyclic redundancy checks (CRC) that are used in communication protocols, data integrity detects not only random modifications (that are introduced for example by physical errors like unstable cable connections), but also malicious modifications that are performed on purpose by a malicious device or user.

In general, the security goal integrity can be further refined. Using security technologies it can be possible to detect which part of the data was modified. Usually, in the communication domain, these further refinements are ignored, instead, a data message is discarded, if the integrity check is invalid. Integrity as a security goal can be provided by cryptographic signatures that need cryptographic keys. Often, integrity is combined with authenticity and encryption. A key exchange at the beginning of the communication allows to exchange keys that are not only used for encryption, but also to preserve the integrity of the transmitted data.

2.2.3 Availability

Availability describes another aspect of computer security. In general, full availability requires a service to be online and ready to serve requests at all times without interruptions. This includes the service's responsiveness to service requests and timely responses. Beside the obvious requirements like power and network connectivity (if the service is network-based), this security goal is more difficult to achieve, if the number of service queries grows. Even a server-based service cannot service all requests, when the network connection queue is blocked with queries. Similarly, the type of service may influence the availability, e.g., when the number of queries grows exponentially with the number of service users.

In the pervasive computing domain, the availability security goal can be reached by service and device distribution. A more federated and distributed architecture of services allows by design the service to be more scalable. It should be noted however, that some service endpoints of a distributed service might be unavailable for some time. I.e., although the service in general is available, not all service data might be available all the time, which might effect the service quality negatively. This is especially true for the pervasive computing domain since it supports many resource-constrained devices like smartphones, which might be not available, for example because of their mobility (they moved to another environment) or because of energy savings. Similarly, these devices can be attacked more easily by malicious devices or users, because of their constrained resources. A powerful device (which in the context of sensors or smartphones could be even a notebook) can block communication or occupy the service with requests (a denial of service). This might interrupt access to a service in this area, but cannot disable the service completely, because of the distributed nature of the pervasive computing domain.

In summary, the availability security goal is already covered by design in the pervasive computing domain. Any changes to the design of pervasive applications should therefore make sure that they do not introduce single points of failure or similar design mistakes that reduce the effectiveness of availability by design.

2.2.4 Authenticity

This security goal describes that a user or device can be authenticated successfully. For peer-to-peer device interactions, it allows to identify the communication partners. Additionally, it can also mean to authenticate the current user of a device. Examples would be a user authentication via a password or by the use of biometrics such as fingerprints. In this context, user authentication usually requires user participation. Device authentication on the other hand can run fully automated, but lacks the additional user identification. If a device is lost by its owner, the automated authentication deployed on the device might still be able to authenticate properly, but the device itself could be in the hands of a user with malicious intents. As a result, different security levels can be established that require different levels of authenticity. Also, revoking a device's authentication should be foreseen.

The authentication of a user or a device is usually a requirement for role-based access control or other access control mechanisms. In this case, the user or device must be properly authenticated, before accessing restricted resources. Only after successful authentication, the user is searched for in the user database and possible access rights are granted. The authenticity of devices is often required to successfully execute a key exchange at the start of the communication. Before (symmetric) keys for encryption and integrity are assigned to a connection, the device is authenticated, effectively authenticating every further message of a connection (and not only one device). Using asymmetric cryptography, messages can be authenticated by one communication partner, this is often used in client-server interactions, where only one partner (usually the server) needs to prove his authenticity. The pervasive computing domain consists of many peer-to-peer interactions that may need the authenticity of both communication partners for a secure interaction.

2.2.5 Privacy

The concept of privacy first appears similar to confidentiality, as the goal is that private data should stay private. But the concept goes further and includes the idea that data should not be shared with third parties, if not required. These third parties may include third party service providers, even when the data to these service providers is secured properly (by means of encryption, integrity and authentication). The general idea is to not share (private) data, if it is not required. A service may require sharing private data to provide its functionality. For example, if the device uses a service to search for nearby devices, the service will require the current position of the device to provide this service. By keeping the data private, privacy protects a user from the unwanted release and use of private data by third parties at the cost of service quality.

If the data is not shared at all, this would result in perfect privacy, but might result in bad query results when third party services are used. While data obfuscation might help by protecting the user's privacy, data that is obfuscated too much will result in a bad service experience for the user, while sharing all data will result in a good service, but might endanger a user's privacy. Often, each user has a different perception on how her personal privacy policy should be shaped. Therefore, many pervasive applications include the creation of privacy policies or settings. Each user can individualize these policies, which might result in a match of her personal privacy. In this thesis, we try to keep the user in control of her privacy by not sharing data with third parties, but by keeping the data on the user's own devices, whenever possible.

2.3 Applications

The pervasive computing domain has a number of context-based applications. Examples are CenceMe [MLF+08], Living++, a platform for assisted living [IFW+13] or indoor localization [WHZM13]. Most of these applications use and share context which can contain private information. The security goals described previously are often disregarded during the development of pervasive applications.

Besides the sharing of context, pervasive applications often also implement or use other features or components such as context distribution, role assignment and access control. All these components must be designed with security and privacy in mind, preventing malicious devices or users to take control. Although each application usually defines an individual scenario including an individual attack model that may differ from standard security models, the pervasive computing domain might exhibit a common model which was introduced by the use of a pervasive middleware that is shared among pervasive application. The pervasive middleware is a common point of attack that needs to be secured properly.

In the following, we will describe two European projects that developed a pervasive middleware. The middleware was evaluated with different real-world example applications that each included components for secure (context-based) interactions. The author of this thesis was involved in the development of the middleware and the example applications that are presented here and in the following chapters.

2.3.1 PECES

The PECES project (PErvasive Computing in Embedded Systems) [PEC10] has been focusing on the creation of a software layer for the cooperation of embedded devices across smart spaces in a context-dependent, secure and trustworthy manner. The project developed and implemented a pervasive middleware. The PECES middleware features spontaneous interactions and

Figure 2.7: PECES: Smart Car using a Smart Parking Lot

bridges communication technologies. Additionally, it contains context and role distribution services and enables secure (group) communication. The middleware can create so-called smart spaces that can be used for spontaneous pervasive interactions.

In contrast to other pervasive scenarios, PECES was focused on overcoming the islands of integration, i.e., bridging the communication between different smart spaces such as smart homes or smart offices. One possible solution to this is the hierarchical role assignment that is described in Chapter 5. To be applicable to a broad range of pervasive scenarios, the PECES middleware targets different device types, from resource-constrained devices such as sensors, routers or smartphones to notebooks, PCs and servers. All these devices can be integrated into a smart space and interact with each other, regardless of the used communication technology. To enable rapid application prototyping, several development tools were created that allow the developer to create pervasive applications, easily.

The PECES project implemented also application prototypes that were tested in Valencia, Spain, in Szeged, Hungary and in Newcastle, UK. An example smart car application is shown in Figure 2.7. Here, a smart car has just left a smart parking lot and the billing information is presented on the screen of the navigation system. This scenario shows the integration of different *smart islands* (the smart car and the smart parking lot) into one overarching smart space.

The PECES project provides a very good example for the use of a middleware in the integration of isolated smart spaces and shows that the peer-to-peer model can be used even for service interactions in the pervasive computing domain.

2.3.2 GAMBAS

The GAMBAS project (Generic Adaptive Middleware for Behavior-driven Autonomous Services) [GAM12] had been created as a successor project of PECES. The focus of PECES was more on services and their interactions as well as the integration of isolated smart spaces. After solving these technical difficulties, the GAMBAS project aimed at the extension of the middleware developed in PECES with a more user-centric approach. In the end, the user's context should be utilized for autonomously adapting pervasive applications or services while preserving the user's privacy.

One of the main goals of the GAMBAS project is to fulfill the vision of distraction-free task support for users in the pervasive computing domain. Only constant adaption by detecting the user's intents and context can help to achieve this goal. If – at the same time – the user's privacy should be preserved, innovative privacy-preserving techniques must be developed and integrated into the GAMBAS middleware. An example of this is shown in Chapter 6. Besides this, the GAMBAS middleware also developed several context, intent and activity recognizers that supported the adaptation. Because of its user-centric goal, a user interface was created that runs directly on the user's smartphone. Nevertheless, the GAMBAS middleware is still supporting the whole range of pervasive devices, starting from sensors to servers, similar to the PECES middleware.

The GAMBAS project created several application prototypes that are available worldwide in the public area of the Google Play store (supported by Android smartphones). A focus lied on the city of Madrid, Spain that features a bus navigation application build completely by GAMBAS technology. An example screen is shown in Figure 2.8. It shows the map of Madrid while using public transport with additional information such as the current bus line the user is located in, the final stop and the number of stops the user has to stay in the bus. Additionally to this visual information, the user can use his headphones to get spoken instructions for his bus trip. Also, the user may use voice commands for interacting with the application.

Figure 2.8: GAMBAS: Bus Navigator Trip in Madrid

Another application developed by the GAMBAS project is shown in Figure 2.9. It provides a service to the users of public transport as well as the public transport operator by showing the crowd level of buses in Madrid. The crowd level is detected by routers deployed in the buses that are connected to the crowd service located at the university of Duisburg-Essen. The routers detect the activity of the bus users' smartphones and estimate the number of people in a bus. The figure presented here shows the crowd level of buses on a Monday, green lines mark uncrowded bus routes while orange or red lines imply a higher crowd level.

The GAMBAS project shows how a pervasive middleware can help the user in fulfilling his everyday user tasks. Using context and activity recognition as well as speech input, the middleware is distraction-free to the user. As we will outline in the Chapters 6 and 7, the GAMBAS middleware also protects the user's privacy.

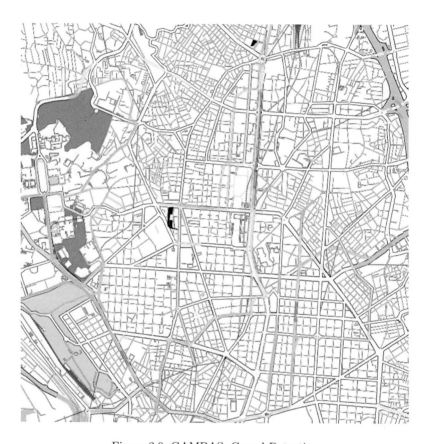

Figure 2.9: GAMBAS: Crowd Detection

3 System Support for Security and Privacy in Pervasive Computing

While many pervasive middleware systems make extensive use of context or role assignment, often security mechanisms are not considered, not implemented or only marked as future work. Only some of these approaches describe ideas for security or privacy. Here, we will discuss related work, identify gaps and derive requirements with a focus on both common, non-security goals of context and role management in a pervasive computing domain as well as on security-related goals. The requirements can then later be used to evaluate our work that we describe in the Chapters 4 to 7.

3.1 Related Work

The chapter is subdivided into different sections that each represent topics relevant to the area of pervasive computing. We will first describe more general related work such as infrastructure type and environment boundaries and their security issues. Then, we will focus on different aspects of security such as context privacy, trust, secure key-exchanges and context privacy policies. In each of the sections, we will try to identify possible gaps which will then help us to derive general requirements in the following subsection.

3.1.1 Type of Pervasive Infrastructure

The most common design approach for context management taken by existing middleware systems for pervasive computing is to rely on a centralized – and possibly hierarchically organized – infrastructure [BDR07]. To name a few, Korpipää et al. [KM03] propose a framework that utilizes a centralized server to store context information for clients. The service-oriented middleware proposed by Gu et al. [GPZ05] also relies on a centralized context interpreter for gathering context data from distributed context providers which can then be provided to various clients. Similarly, CASS [FC04] relies on a central database to store context information from sensor listeners of remote clients. Such centralized approaches may introduce bottlenecks and introduce a single point of trust with the associated privacy implications (the centralized server must be fully trusted, a security breach might make all stored context information publicly available). To overcome the first problem, CoBrA [CFJ04] enables the federation of several servers, however, it does not handle the latter. Existing decentralized solutions such as [DAS01] or [HSP+03] usually rely on much simpler models for context and they do not consider security and privacy.

In many cases, the type of infrastructure that is chosen also has implications on the privacy of context information. A primary obstacle for securing privacy is the aforementioned centralization of pervasive infrastructures, which also includes the centralization of context management. Al-Muhtadi et al. [AMHCM06] secures context information in such a centralized manner. Context is here encrypted using symmetric group keys and a central server in the GAIA environment en- and decrypts the context information. Accessing the encrypted data will be possible, if the central server can verify the needed context information. GAIA uses a centralized server for data storage and access control. All data encryptions that are performed by the mobile devices are based on symmetric group keys. Furthermore, the context based data will be en- and decrypted by the central server, which also determines the current context of all devices. This central server must therefore be trusted, because it can read the context information of all devices. A more distributed system architecture would possibly overcome this. Additionally, symmetric group keys are usually problematic, if (mobile) group members join and leave groups spontaneously, like in peer-to-peer networks. Each group key must then be re-created and the context information must be first decrypted with the old key and then encrypted with the new key. For peer-to-peer networks, a per device scheme would be more flexible to the spontaneous formation of groups. Additionally, the data should be allowed to be distributed through the whole network, so every device would carry the data while preserving data integrity. In this case, also the verification of context information needs to be distributed and every device in the network would then be able to validate context information.

In addition to centralized approaches, some authors also tried to use context information-based security mechanisms in a decentralized fashion. Robinson et al. [RB04] creates a shared secret which depends on the room acoustics. As a result, the infrastructure would consist of several separated islands that each group the devices in a room. Every device in a room should have the same key since they are creating the key at the same time. To ensure that the key is identical, the devices must be time-synchronized with a very high precision. Additionally, the idea depends on the assumption that the room acoustics is almost the same, independent from the place where the device is located in the room. While this could be the case in some rooms, such as in office buildings, not all rooms fulfill this special condition. The authors suggest a periodical re-keying, to re-enable the communication with devices which (mis-)calculated a different key. This key can only be used to secure communication in a room, not to securely communicate across different rooms, for example to secure communication within a company.

Most approaches described here are not suitable for peer-to-peer networks. Because – in this scenario – no central servers are available, they require a decentralized infrastructure. Also, there does not exist a single point of trust and it should be possible to use arbitrary types of context within the infrastructure. Additionally, to maintain the distributed architecture of the pervasive computing domain, the context verification should be possible by every device in a domain in contrast to having a single trusted server that needs to perform all secure context interactions. If required, the distributed context validation should also be possible inter-domain.

3.1.2 Environment Boundaries

Most existing middleware systems for pervasive computing exploit locality to improve their performance. To do this, they configure the execution environment by introducing logical boundaries that reduce the number of interacting devices. Usually, these boundaries are defined on the basis of proximity or location depending on the underlying system model.

We see pervasive computing environments as so-called *smart spaces* that could include an arbitrary set of devices. Other middleware systems that support smart spaces such as IROS [PJKF03], GAIA [RHC+02], EasyLiving [BMK+00], Aura [GSS02] or Oxygen [Rud01] are usually bound to a specific geographic location. This location may represent a building such as a home or a work place [BMK+00], [Rud01] or a single room such as a meeting room or an office [RHC+02], [PJKF03], [GSS02], [YGG+03]. Within this area, a coordinating server is responsible for providing additional services such as shared persistent storage, context management or application configuration, for example. Thereby, the server is responsible for dynamically handling the mobile devices that enter or leave the area. However, without additional mechanisms, these systems cannot cross the boundaries of the area and are based on a server infrastructure.

Middleware systems that support smart peers such as BASE [HBS03] and PCOM [BHSR04] or MundoCore [AKM07], for instance, usually rely on different proximity metrics. With these metrics they define the boundaries around each device, for example, as the set of devices in n-hop neighborhood [RJH02]. Similarly, concepts such as abstract regions [WM04] and scenes [KJ07] use location as reference point to form dynamic environments around it. For defining the boundaries, these approaches are limited to topological or geographical regions. Logical neighborhoods [MP06] and Hood [WSBC04] are two approaches that restrict the scope to the physical (i.e., 1-hop) neighborhood.

To allow developers to address the specific regions in a network, Spatial Views [NKI03] provides a programmable abstraction over different properties of the underlying network. Similarly, in Regiment [NW04], the developer views the complete network as geographical or topological streams and she can manipulate these streams to address a region. The above approaches are useful in defining the pervasive environment in immediate vicinity. Enviro-Track [ABC$^+$04], targets towards application tracking, goes beyond physical closeness and focuses on data centric communication between entities with similar context. However, these approaches do not support environment composition.

Approaches that support the composability of different smart spaces are UbicKids [MYA$^+$05] and Super Spaces [ACC04]. UbicKids provides mechanisms for enabling cross pervasive environment communication by exposing services to the existing UbicKids pervasive environments. Super Spaces utilize active spaces [RHC$^+$02] that are by themselves based on geographic locations. Thus, they are an additional mechanism that has been applied to extend the boundaries of the underlying smart space.

Environment configuration should be able to naturally support these cases without additional mechanisms. In addition, it should also support other notions of context-dependent environments, i.e., environments for arbitrarily formed smart spaces, regardless of the geographical location. In the end, this allows to create smart spaces which can span an arbitrary big area. Using a pervasive middleware, it should be possible to make environmental boundaries freely configurable and composable, allowing to form hierarchical groups of smart spaces, if required. Additionally, the boundaries of such a smart space should allowed to be defined in a flexible manner, meaning not only dependent on physical boundaries such as rooms or floors, but instead allowing any type of context information to define the boundaries of a smart space.

3.1.3 Context and Role Privacy and Security

In general, roles could be regarded as an overlay on context, i.e., they represent the next hierarchical level. This allows the role to be seen as context itself. Using this perspective, it is clear that roles must be secured as well as the context information they are based on. We will first present approaches for context security and privacy (which also apply to roles) and will then shortly discuss access control using context or roles.

While many authors mention context privacy as an important goal for future work in their middleware [HIMB05, NGMW08, DAS01, SFH09], only few really address this problem, for example Hong et al. [HL04], who describe an architecture for privacy-sensitive ubiquitous computing and Kang et al. [KLJ+08] who does not provide further details about the actual security implementation.

We agree with Hong et al. [HL04] that sensitive context information should be stored decentralized, on a device owned by the user. Additionally, we think that context privacy requires security, so integrity and authenticity of context as well as encrypted communication should be an integral part of a pervasive computing infrastructure. Most peer-to-peer security schemes use a certificate architecture that is mutually trusted by all devices [Wal02]. This creates a single authority that is responsible for the devices in the complete network. It would be more flexible to allow each device to decide which other devices (and possibly infrastructures) should be trusted. This allows to deny devices the access to sensitive information, by adding these devices (and possibly all other, unknown devices) to a list of untrusted devices.

Also other centralized approaches such as GAIA [AMHCM06] or Vigil [KUP+02] try to secure context information. GAIA uses central services whereas Vigil utilizes agents. Vigil uses certificates for devices in the environment. Their environments (SmartSpaces) each consist of a Service Manager that announces public services and is used by devices to register with the environment. All Service Managers are organized in a tree-structure and have trust relationships established with each other. Similarly, each SmartSpace has a Security Agent that is responsible for the secure service access in the environment. Although this scenario is more flexible with regard to the validation of security, a peer-to-peer approach could completely omit central authorities or devices, instead, every device could validate certificates, roles and context on behalf of another device, if they have previously agreed on working together and established a trust relationship. As described before, GAIA uses central servers for access control and for data storage. All data is stored (encrypted) on a central server that verifies certain requirements (e.g., context), before the data can be accessed by a device. In a peer-to-peer network the data could be stored on each device individually and also the access to services could be controlled by the device executing the service itself. This would result in decentralized context security where central authorities would not be needed.

PACE [HIMB05] introduces an access control system based on *situations*. Since situations are usually defined through context information, the system does not preserve privacy if the context is not protected from being tampered. A first step towards the creation of a secure access control mechanism should therefore be the creation of a context management that protects the context's integrity and authenticity. An extension for their middleware [HWMI05] bounds the privacy of context information to the *owners* of the context that can define privacy settings. The context server must then follow these privacy settings while handling the context. We agree with Henricksen et al. that one step towards securing context requires context traceability (who issued/detected the context) and therefore each context should have an owner. This could be realized by assigning a source and a target device to each context element, which would be similar to the owner concept. The central context server stands in contrast to our concept of peer-to-peer-based pervasive smart spaces. We envision a system where no central, trusted server is needed.

Focusing more on privacy-awareness, Ni et al. [NBL+10] describe an extensive framework to model role-based access control. It allows to assign roles based on hierarchical and conditional constraints. One gap that we identified in this work is that they are not considering how roles or context are being secured if they are exchanged over an insecure communication channel.

Summarized, context and role privacy needs to be secured properly, regardless of the type of context or role that needs to be secured. Additionally, the security should be reliable and be suitable for devices in peer-to-peer networks.

3.1.4 Trust

Trust in users or devices is an important concept. Trust reduces the number of devices that interact with each other depending on the required level of trust (or security) of the used pervasive service(s) or application(s). A simple trust model would be a certificate-based notion of trust that only trusts devices of a certain certificate domain such as in a company. For peer-to-peer pervasive domains, several other approaches to express trust were suggested.

Kagal et al. [KFJ01] distributes trust to devices of a foreign domain by using the personnel that is working in the domain as room managers. These managers can grant other persons or devices the same rights that they currently own in this room. So a manager could allow a guest device to use the office printer that he is also allowed to use. Personal trust is used as a substitute for secure context information. Also, the room managers are responsible for granting their access rights to someone else. In general, we do not consider that depending on personal trust is superior in comparison with the use of security tokens such as secured context information or roles, especially when considering social engineering.

Lagesse et al. [LKPW09] describes a reputation-based trust system. Our understanding of peer-to-peer pervasive environments requires that trust values are stored on each device individually and that there should be no central trust group formed. Reputation-based systems [KNS05, Ser04] can be misused by attackers. If attackers use a device that behaves well until it reaches a high reputation level, it is possible to modify the trust relationships to their needs. The use of certificate hierarchies would avoid these kind of attacks, because a valid certificate is needed before trusted interactions are possible. Nevertheless, a combination of different trust models could be beneficial. The trust model should therefore be extensible and it should be possible to add reputation-based trust on top of other implemented trust models such as a certificate-based trust model.

Another approach to model trust relationships for role-based access control is shown by Takabi et al. [TAJ07]. Here, fuzzy relation equations are used to describe the trust in users. Roles can require a particular trust level, before they are assigned. In our vision, the secure role assignment may have additional constraints about the context's source and freshness, but not necessarily about the trust in the role's target devices. This enhances the seamless transition between environments. Consider a device which is currently located in a remote environment. It may still be allowed to access services there, if it is in possession of the required context. Instead of adding a different parameter (i.e., trust) to roles, we would suggest that trust constraints are modeled with regard to context.

3.1.5 Secure Key-exchange

A secure key-exchange is often a requirement before secure communication can take place. When a pervasive environment is formed, secure keys are required for example for the assignment of roles that are used for role-based access control. Similarly, secure keys are needed for secure communication between the different devices in the environments. If they are properly exchanged by the devices or users in the environment, they can even be used for device or user authentication.

To provide user-level authentication, some approaches use server-based context-detection as the mechanism to allow or deny access to resources [AMHCM06,TAK+04]. As described previously, pervasive environments are peer-based and can therefore not rely on a central server. Of course, a key-exchange mechanism may use third-party infrastructure (i.e., online services) to establish shared and user-level keys. In [SS13] and [RB04] the authors describe how context, such as microphone recordings, can be used directly to create a shared key between devices. According to them, this works well inside buildings, but ceases to work properly if used outside. A pervasive environment requires a reliable secure key-exchange that can be used both indoors and outdoors. Using context data from the smartphone's sensors also exhibits scalability issues. Imagine sensor data from an accelerometer which needs devices to be shaken together (up to a duration of 20s) such that the accelerometer detects (almost) identical data. Smart-Its friends [HMS+01] and similar approaches [BSHL07,MG07] generate a key based on this data. However, this approach is only feasible for a small amount of devices.

The combination of different context features for key-exchanges is presented by PINtext [SSJ12] or Mayrhofer et al. [May07]. While enhancing security by combining context features, this also combines their disadvantages, e.g., using the accelerometer and the microphone at the same time requires shaking the devices *and* constrains the key-exchange to indoor locations. Although these approaches do not need an Internet connection, context dependent key-exchanges need precise time synchronization between devices. In a pervasive environment, resource-poor devices might not have a reliable clock source and can exhibit a drift. A key-exchange mechanism should not require a precise time synchronization before the exchange can take place, instead, a time-shift of several minutes should be tolerable.

Other mechanisms to perform a key-exchange are based on near field communication (NFC) technology. In the Bluetooth specification [Blu07], NFC is mentioned as a possible mechanism to pair devices. Suomalainen et al. [SVA07] show that NFC can be used for the negotiation of keys for other network types, mostly because direct proximity (usually 1–10 cm) is required for successful communication in NFC. Some authors describe the inherent security of NFC for man-in-the-middle attacks [HB06], but show that eavesdropping can be done easily. Others point out possible security and privacy breaches, for example by using a unique id [MLKS08]. Although NFC is usually used for short-range communication, Francis et al. [FHMM10] describe a relay attack that can be used to circumvent this limitation.

Besides this device-centric approach, it should be possible to exchange keys on a per user basis. Additionally, when keys are exchanged beforehand, they can be used directly, when the interaction takes place and would be immune to attacks that rely on a specific communication technology and are executed during the interaction. As a result, a key that was exchanged beforehand could be used for any communication technology, including NFC. Nevertheless, establishing group keys using NFC still needs physical interaction between devices which, as mentioned before, does not scale. ProxiMate [MMV+11] is another key-exchange protocol that retrieves a shared key from RF signals. To obtain a key, it is necessary to put the pairing devices into physical proximity, similar to NFC. According to the authors, the protocol is resistant to attackers that are more than 6.2 cm away (at 2.4 GHz). The protocol could be used to exchange a shared key between devices, but it might be impossible to put all users' devices in the necessary proximity, if the number of devices is too large. Since the number of devices in pervasive environments may vary, a secure key-exchange mechanism should be highly scalable and should not have constraints on the number of devices, be able to create group and user-level keys and run fully automated.

In SPATE [LSH+09], a small group of users is able to exchange a key by comparing hash codes (the so-called T-Flags). This enables SPATE to establish a key for secure interaction at additional costs, i.e., all users have to recognize and compare the T-Flag images. To start the key-exchange process, SPATE requires the initiating device to scan a bar-code from all other devices' displays (requiring a built-in camera on each device and retrieving the devices' network addresses). Since SPATE also needs the number of group members typed in manually, SPATE and related approaches like Seeing-is-believing [MPR05] and GAnGS [CCK+08] need manual configuration, while a key-exchange in a pervasive environment requires an automatic key-exchange.

Many existing key-exchange mechanisms need an Internet connection during the key-exchange phase and they use a different service provider for authentication purposes. Examples are OpenID [Ope07] and OAuth [HL10, Har12].

While OpenID allows the user to use one account for several different services and service providers, OAuth creates an access token, mostly used by applications that want to access a service on behalf of the user. A service that uses OpenID needs to trust the service that provides the account creation and authorization. The latter is therefore a trusted third-party that is actively involved in the authorization process. In contrast, using the OAuth process, the user actively grants rights from a service to another. Usually, the granted rights are displayed to the user and must be confirmed manually. A key-exchange for peer-to-peer-based pervasive environments should not require a trusted third party that authorizes users or devices. Additionally, when the communication takes place, no Internet connectivity might be available, i.e., it might be necessary to exchange keys before the communication takes place.

For secure key-exchanges in pervasive environments, we see three main gaps. First, a secure key-exchange should easily scale to hundreds of collaboration partners. Second, it should support to provide user-level as opposed to device-level authentication. Third, it should not require Internet connectivity during the interaction, i.e., the key should be available without an active Internet connection.

3.1.6 Individual Privacy Policy

An individual privacy policy reflects the idea that each user might have different views about her personal privacy. As such, it might be necessary to create a privacy policy that is individual for each user. It could be possible to exploit the sharing of information (i.e., context) that the user is already performing with other users of online collaboration tools (such as Facebook or Google Calendar) here. In the end, the individual privacy policy should answer the question which kind of data should be shared with whom.

This question becomes increasingly important, since there are more and more pervasive computing applications that share context information. An example is the CenceMe [MLF+08] application which shares detected context. While currently these applications usually post directly to the online collaboration tools and use a user-defined policy for each of them, a privacy policy generator would allow them to use one consistent privacy policy for multiple online collaboration tools with several context types.

Policy Language

Several papers describe approaches to create or extend a privacy policy language [KFJ03, HYS05, W3C06]. Since there is no default privacy policy language, any approach to create an individual privacy policy should be agnostic to the used privacy policy language, i.e., it should be possible to change the underlying privacy policy language. This would also allow to use a more sophisticated policy language which can be used to describe more complex situations, e.g., if a context should be shared only in a specific time-slot. Policies could be exported or could convert the created policy to other policy languages, if necessary.

Policy Derivation and Creation

Toch et al. [TSH10] and Fang et al. [FL10] describe that it is difficult for users to adjust their privacy settings to their needs properly. As a consequence, they try to help them and ease the process of creating the privacy settings for online collaboration tools. Fang et al. [FL10] create a privacy wizard that can be trained by the user and allows to configure (at least parts of) the user's privacy settings automatically. Toch et al. [TSH10] analyze and cluster existing privacy settings, allowing a new user to choose from a popular set of privacy settings instead of starting from scratch. This allows users to set their privacy settings correctly, which is mandatory when the settings are used to generate an individual privacy policy out of the privacy settings. Both approaches do not extract or create an individual privacy policy from online collaboration tools or detect the context type that is shared, but they provide additional help to users. Since these approaches might result in a better representation of the user's wishes (with regard to privacy settings), this can result in an even better fit for an individual privacy policy that is generated by using sharing settings from online collaboration tools.

There also exists related work that is deriving privacy policies from online collaboration tools [Dan09, VSCY09, Toc14]. Danezis [Dan09] is focusing on the relationships between the users. They are grouping them according to the mutual relationships and because of this relationship, a context is assigned to them. Here, the context describes the group and not the type of data that is shared. Additionally, the user specified sharing settings of shared resources are not taken into account. Vyas et al. [VSCY09] tries to automatically manage privacy for different types of content. Instead of using machine learning techniques to derive the context information, they require the user to manually assign *tags* to the content they are going to share.

While this will work on user-published content like a Blog post, average users of online collaboration tools might not be willing to tag all their posts or events. Additionally, this contradicts the concept of pervasive computing to automate as many tasks as possible. Toch [Toc14] describes how privacy preferences can be crowd-sourced using a crowdsourcing framework called *Super-Ego*. Besides crowdsourcing privacy preferences, they also predict the preferences (using the crowd sourced data). They are using a centralized server to store manually made privacy preference decisions in a so-called crowd model. For a pervasive environment, it would be necessary to use several context sources from online collaboration tools, not using the crowd, but only one, individual user. Then, a privacy policy could be generated that represents the individual preferences of this user. Using the peer-to-peer nature of pervasive networks, it would make sense to store the individual privacy policy exclusively on the user's own device and make it available to other pervasive computing applications that are executed on the same device.

3.2 Requirements for Security and Privacy in Pervasive Computing

We are briefly revisiting the related work sub-sections to identify the gaps that are used to form general requirements for security and privacy in pervasive computing.

Regarding the type of infrastructure, we envision pervasive environments or smart spaces to be based on peer-to-peer devices. As such, the structure of the network is **decentralized**. This decentralization also includes the possibilities for each device to act as a context verification device, i.e., each device can verify context information, if required. Additionally, although the number of devices in smart spaces may vary, the total number of devices that interact in pervasive scenarios can be high. As a result, the infrastructure should be **highly scalable**. When a pervasive infrastructure is based on context information, it should be possible to extend it easily and to adapt it to new context types, if necessary. Therefore, the infrastructure should support **generic context types**.

Pervasive environments – in general – do not have any boundaries. While this would allow each device to contact another device, regardless of its (geographical) position, it can make sense to introduce logical boundaries. These boundaries may be introduced by so-called smart spaces or pervasive environments that support a smaller number of devices. To enable interactions between pervasive applications even when boundaries of pervasive environments are defined, it is necessary that these boundaries are **configurable** and can be adapted to different pervasive scenarios. Additionally, the boundaries should be **flexible**, i.e., can be based on different types of context information and should not be restricted to the geographical location only. Allowing interactions between these pervasive environment is important to overcome the issue of isolated islands that cannot communicate with each other. As such, the environments must be **composable** in a way that allows the interaction between them.

Protecting context information or roles in pervasive environments is an important goal for bringing security and privacy to the pervasive computing domain. Any mechanism that tries to achieve this goal, needs to be **generic** with regard to the type of context or role that should be protected. This allows the addition of new types of context or roles without changing the protection mechanism. The protection itself should be **reliably secure**. The level of security depends on the pervasive scenario, but in general, Internet-level grade of security should be provided, since often, remote interactions are mediated over the Internet.

In peer-to-peer networks, trust in devices can be expressed in many different ways. Because of the decentralized nature of the pervasive computing domain, trust domains should also be **decentralized**. Additionally, the trust model should be **extensible** with other mechanisms to allow later extensions.

Before devices in a pervasive environment can communicate securely with each other, a cryptographic key must be established. Because of the possibly high number of devices in such an environment, the key-exchange should be **highly scalable**. Often, the interaction of devices is not a pure machine-to-machine interaction. As a result, **user-level authentication** is required during the key exchange. When the interaction takes place, Internet connectivity might not be available for all communication partners. The exchanged **keys** should therefore be **available** when the interaction takes place, independent of an active Internet connection.

When context is shared between devices or users by a pervasive application, an individual privacy policy is necessary to preserve the user's privacy. The policy restricts the sharing. A privacy policy generator needs to be **generic** to the kind of context that is supported by the generator and the policy. Additionally, the generator should be as **automated** as possible to preserve

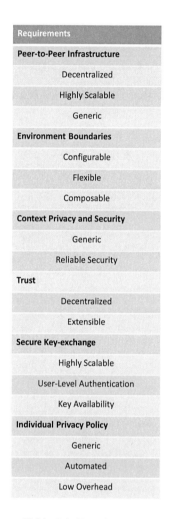

Requirements
Peer-to-Peer Infrastructure
Decentralized
Highly Scalable
Generic
Environment Boundaries
Configurable
Flexible
Composable
Context Privacy and Security
Generic
Reliable Security
Trust
Decentralized
Extensible
Secure Key-exchange
Highly Scalable
User-Level Authentication
Key Availability
Individual Privacy Policy
Generic
Automated
Low Overhead

Table 3.1: Requirements

the distraction-free pervasive environment. A privacy policy that is generated on a smartphone also needs to exhibit a **low overhead** in terms of resource usage (CPU time and network bandwidth).

In the following chapters, we will first discuss an approach for context security, then our work on secure role assignment. After this, we will discuss a possible solution for secure key-exchanges in pervasive environments. Finally, we discuss an approach for the generation of an individual privacy policy. During these chapters, we will fill the identified gaps and follow the requirements that we have derived here and that are visible in Table 3.1. All the approaches that are presented in the following chapters are then evaluated against the derived requirements in Chapter 8.

4 Peer-based Context Management

In this chapter, we describe our contribution to peer-based context management. First, we present our approach for the privacy-preserving context management. Providing adequate support for context acquisition and management is a non-trivial task that complicates application development. While many middleware systems rely on a centralized context service that must be trusted by its users, our approach is peer-based and therefore privacy-preserving. Second, we show our secure context distribution framework that is used to distribute context securely to trusted or even non-trusted devices. This enhances our privacy-preserving context management with the ability to gather context from many different trusted or untrusted infrastructures or even independent sensors.

4.1 Privacy-Preserving Context Management

In this section, we describe our approach for privacy-preserving context management. It can be used to gather and query for context information used in ubiquitous computing applications. Here, we show that it is applicable to many different device types, from resource-constrained sensors to desktop PCs or servers. We also describe the privacy-preserving capabilities of our peer-based approach in detail.

4.1.1 Preliminaries

Privacy-preserving context management is necessary to provide users with seamless and distraction-free task support while at the same time their private information is kept private. For ubiquitous computing applications, context management is a requirement since they need information about their current context to provide this type of task support to users. Therefore, they must be able to perceive their context. To avoid repetitive development effort for context management at the application layer, existing middleware systems for ubiquitous computing provide context management support as one of their main building blocks. Thereby, they usually rely on a central system service that manages the context of all devices that are located within a certain physically limited area [BDR07]. Sensors and other devices that are located within the area report their information directly to this service which can then provide a comprehensive view to interested applications. Such a centralized approach can considerably reduce the application development effort. Yet, if the number of devices increases, the central service may become a bottleneck.

While scalability issues can be countered by adding more resources, hierarchical [CFJ04] or decentralized context management [DAS01,HSP+03], from a user's perspective, a more problematic issue resulting from centralization is privacy. Given that context information may reveal sensitive information, centralized context management is only viable in cases where users are willing to put a sufficiently high degree of trust in the intentions and capabilities of the operator. While this might be appropriate for some scenarios such as smart class rooms or smart homes, it is clearly not the case when considering scenarios such as smart shopping malls in which shop owners might operate context management services for their customers. Here, we show how such privacy problems can be avoided by peer-based context management. To validate the approach, we have implemented it on top of the BASE [HWS+10] middleware and used it for application development in the PECES project. This approach should provide a high flexibility while being applicable to a broad spectrum of devices.

4.1.2 Context Model

As basis for a generic context model, we adopt OWL-based context modeling [CFJ04,GWPZ04] since it facilitates autonomicity and interoperability. This enables the usage of an ontology to establish a common understanding among application developers and processing engines. Furthermore, it is possible to reuse existing ontologies such as SOUPA [CPFJ04] or CONON [ZGW05] and it is easy to create extensions to support different application domains. In the following, we outline the underlying technologies and describe how they can be used to define and execute queries.

Since OWL is a vocabulary extension of RDF[1], the atomic data element for context information is an RDF triple. Every piece of context information is implicitly or explicitly represented as a set of triples. To avoid inconsistency of RDF blank nodes in distributed settings, we do not use blank nodes to

---

[1]http://www.w3.org/TR/rdf-syntax/

model context information. Assume there is an infinite set I of Internation-alized Resource Identifiers IRIs and an infinite set L of RDF literals. A triple $(s, p, o) \in (I) \times (I) \times (I \cup L)$ is called a non-blank node RDF triple, where s is the subject, p is the predicate and o is the object. The assertion a triple states that some relationship, indicated by the predicate, holds between the subject and object. As examples for such triples consider statements such as 'user' 'has' 'name' or 'sensor' 'reads' 'value'. Conceptually, a set of triples can then be connected along the subjects to create a graph structure. The assertion of such an RDF graph accounts to asserting all the triples in it, so the meaning of an RDF graph is the conjunction (logical AND) of the statements corresponding to all the triples it contains. This enables the formulation of arbitrary expressions such as 'device' 'has' 'sensor', 'sensor' 'reads' 'value' which can then be used by means of complex queries.

As context information is represented as RDF triples, we naturally chose SPARQL query fragments as basis for defining queries. In order to be suit-able for resource-poor embedded devices, however, we only include basic graph matching patterns as well as built-in conditions. Furthermore, we add simple geo spatial extensions to express nearest neighbor as well as range queries analog to the extension *geospatialweb*[2]. Informally, basic graph matching patterns allow us to formulate sequences of triples that may con-tain variables. Upon execution, the variables are bound based on the triples contained in the model. As a simple example, we might query sensors by specifying a pattern consisting of 'x' 'reads' 'y' and 'x' 'is a' 'sensor'. Us-ing built-in conditions, we can restrict the binding of variables to particular values, e.g., 'y' is greater than 5.

Given this model, the query evaluation process is a state machine which can be presented as a query graph [HH07]. The query graph consists of operators that perform operations on their input data to generate output data. After decomposing a query process into smaller operators, it can be shown that all queries are composed from triple pattern operations. Therefore the minimum operators for building a state machine to execute a query is the triple pattern matching operator. Other operators such as ⋈, ∪ and ⊨ can be optionally built as relational JOIN, UNION and SELECTION operators, if needed.

In contrast to other ontology-based context management systems which use central systems to manage context information, we enable the autonomous context management on many devices. This includes resource-constrained devices like smartphones or sensors that are both used in pervasive com-puting scenarios. The context management actions that can be performed on the devices of course vary, depending on their device type and hardware

---

[2]http://code.google.com/p/geospatialweb/

capability. Small devices like sensors are able to host and share context that are relevant to themselves. This could include information about the sensed data or the hardware configuration. Devices with higher hardware capabilities like smartphones are able to manage not only context that is relevant for them, but could also manage context provided from other devices, connecting for example to a *smart car* or a *smart home*. For intensive, large scale compute tasks like context processing and distribution, devices like PCs or servers are used. The computing power they provide allows them to perform all necessary tasks regarding context management.

4.1.3 System Architecture

To avoid the inherent privacy issues of centralized context management approaches, we take a peer-based approach to context management in which each device is managing its own context that can then be shared with other devices on demand by executing remote queries locally. For spontaneous interaction between devices in the vicinity, we are using BASE [HWS+10] as underlying communication middleware. BASE is structured as a minimal extensible micro-broker that is deployed on each device and mediates all interactions. This results in the layered system structure depicted on the left side of Figure 4.1. At the highest layer, application objects and middleware services interact with each other, either locally or remotely, through their local micro-broker. Usually, this interaction is mediated through stub objects that can be generated automatically from interface definitions. Underneath, the micro-broker takes care of providing a uniform interface for device discovery and interaction. To realize this, BASE utilizes an extensible plug-in architecture to abstract from different communication abstractions, protocols and technologies. So, each middleware instance can be configured with different sets of plug-ins and, at runtime, BASE takes care of automatically composing suitable communication stacks. As indicated on the left side of Figure 4.1, the extensions to support peer-based privacy-preserving context management affect all layers of BASE.

The key storage takes care of establishing the identity of a device or a domain in a secure manner. It associates each device with a unique asymmetric key pair that represents its identity as well as a certificate that is signed by a particular domain. Thereby, domains may either represent individual devices as well as individual users or even larger corporations, e.g., by means of hierarchically signed certificates. Avoiding a central point of trust, individual trust levels are associated to the certificates and stored in the key storage to model trust relationships between devices or domains. The certificate's

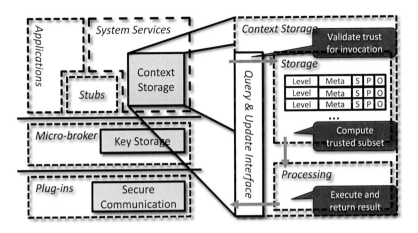

Figure 4.1: Overall Architecture

trust level recursively covers the whole tree spanned by the certificate which reduces configuration effort. The trust levels are only valid for a particular device which enables users to model trust individually. At the same time, it enables the definition of unidirectional relationships. Regarding the trust levels, the key storage does not prescribe a particular semantic. To automate the evaluation of trust relationships, the key storage assumes transitivity such that a higher level of trust includes lower levels. Consequently, the two extremes are **full trust** and **no trust**.

Secure Communication

The extensions for secure communication are verifying and enforcing the sharing according to the trust relationships. Due to the cost of asymmetric cryptography, the certificates contained in the key store are not suitable to secure interactions. Therefore, a key-exchange plug-in negotiates a secure symmetric key using the asymmetric keys. Thereby, the correct trust level is determined by exchanging certificate chains. Once a symmetric key is established and the trust level is evaluated, it is cached to secure all further interactions. This key can then be used by a second plug-in which ensures authenticity, integrity and optionally secrecy. For authenticity and integrity, an HMAC [KBC97] is attached to the transmitted messages. Encryption can be added additionally, e.g., by using AES.

Due to the cost of asymmetric cryptography, the flexible definition of trust relationships using certificates is not suitable to secure interactions. To reduce the resource requirements, a key-exchange plug-in is responsible for negotiating a secure symmetric key using the asymmetric keys. Thereby, it also automatically determines the correct trust level during key exchange by exchanging certificate chains, looking up known (root) certificates in the key storage. Once a symmetric key is established and the trust level is evaluated, it is cached to secure all further interactions. In the spirit of BASE, this is done centrally at the key storage in order to support multiple implementations for key-exchange plug-ins. However, when implementing a key exchange plug-in we found that it is important to rely on optimized cryptographic algorithms to be able to support resource poor devices, a detailed analysis is provided in Section 8.2.2.

Once the key exchange is finished and a cached key is available, it can be used by the second plug-in which ensures authenticity, integrity and optionally secrecy. For authenticity and integrity, the individual messages transmitted between two devices can be secured by attaching a message authentication code. If the underlying communication technology does not provide it already it is furthermore necessary to add encryption. Similarly to the message authentication code, this can be done easily on the basis of the shared symmetric key. By validating the message authentication code and the encryption key, if available, the plug-in ensures that interaction can only be originating from devices which have undergone a key-exchange and can thus be trusted according to the determined level. This knowledge can then be used by the context storage to restrict the access accordingly. As cryptographic primitives, our current implementation relies on a combination of HMAC-SHA1 and AES which introduce only minor costs. A detailed analysis on the performance of our encryption and authentication combination can be found in Chapter 5.

Context Storage

With the extensions described previously, the task of the context storage service is reduced to ensure the generation of query results that adhere to the given trust level. As shown in Figure 4.1, a query and update interface is responsible for accepting incoming queries and update requests. Besides, it is responsible for determining the trust level of the incoming request. For this, it interacts with the key storage to determine the context of the call. The storage part is responsible for storing the context in a generic way that can be supported by resource-constrained devices. As discussed in

Section 4.1.2, we rely on the triple representation defined by RDF [Wora], stored internally in the quoted string representation. To restrict the sharing of context on the basis of trust, each triple is extended with a trust *level*. In addition, each triple may contain further *meta* information to allow the decentralized validation as described later in detail in Section 4.2.

If the call has been issued locally from some application or middleware service, the highest trust level (*full trust*) will be assigned which grants full access to the device's context. If the call has been issued from a remote device, the key storage will reply with any value between *full trust* and *no trust* which is then used to determine the subset of context that may be exposed.

Given this context representation, a caller may add/remove triples with the associated level and meta information to manipulate the device's context. In our implementation, the addition of level information as well as the triple generation for a particular context type is done statically as part of a sensor implementation. When executing a query, the update and query interface uses the attached level information to determine the relevant triples. It selects all triples whose level is lower or equal to the caller's level and forwards them together with the request to the processing engine. The processing engine then executes the query over the set of triples. Since the context that has been used during query evaluation is restricted already, the result can be passed directly to the caller.

4.2 Secure Context Distribution Framework

In this section, we describe how context can be distributed securely. To achieve this goal, we have created a framework that can be run on resource-constrained devices. The class of devices that can execute the framework includes sensors that detect context information such as SunSPOTs. This work complements the privacy-preserving context management that was presented in the previous section. It describes the security mechanisms that are used to securely distribute context information using resource-poor devices in detail.

4.2.1 Preliminaries

Pervasive computing envisions seamless support for everyday user tasks by means of devices that are integrated in the user's environment. Due to their integration, many devices are specialized and resource-poor and due to user and device mobility, the resulting pervasive systems are typically dynamic. As a consequence, many pervasive applications are inherently distributed since a single device alone cannot provide thorough task support. Combined with the dynamics, this creates execution environments that demand a high degree of configurability and adaptability.

In addition to seamlessness, pervasive computing also strives for distraction-free task support. Thus, it is usually not feasible to shift the responsibility of adapting an application to the user. Instead, providing the desired user experience requires the application developer to strike the right balance between manual control and automation. However, the benefit of automation can quickly be nullified by inappropriate decisions. This is especially problematic if the automated decisions may have security implications, e.g., if they may compromise the user's privacy.

To avoid inappropriate decisions, it is often necessary to consider a large number of variables. Besides from technical characteristics of the execution environment such as the available devices and services, a significant set of variables is usually bound to the state of the physical world which is commonly referred to as context information or simply context. Context may entail the location of objects and devices, for example, and it is typically supposed to be gathered unobtrusively by means of embedded sensors. Consequently, it is necessary to ensure the validity of context information that is used for automation.

To ensure the validity, existing systems usually rely on a trusted infrastructure that consists of a centralized context service with permanent secure connections to all relevant sensors. This approach can be applied easily to smart environments since they are often built around a centralized server that manages a single administrative domain. In contrast to that, peer-based systems are typically fully distributed since they cannot rely on the permanent availability of any device. Moreover, they may span devices from several administrative domains which can make it impossible to define a single trustworthy context service.

As a consequence, it is necessary to use the available devices to distribute context information in peer-based systems. However, this approach requires additional precautions to ensure the validity of the context information. Here, we derive the requirements on secure context distribution in peer-based systems. Furthermore, we describe a generic distribution framework to enable the usage of context information in security critical applications. On the basis of a prototypical implementation, we indicate that the proposed framework can achieve a security level that is comparable to a centralized system while being applicable to a broad range of scenarios.

4.2.2 System Model

We are building on the work of [BSGR03] and [HHM09], therefore our work is focused on peer-based pervasive systems. In these systems, devices that are within communication range connect to each other on-the-fly using short-range wireless communication such as Bluetooth or WiFi. Due to miniaturization and specialization, the devices encountered in these systems are often resource-poor. As a result, they need to interact with each other in order to provide thorough support for user tasks. Due to mobility, the available set of devices is continuously fluctuating. Thus, in contrast to smart environments, peer-based systems cannot make use of a central coordinator. Instead, they must coordinate in a decentralized manner.

In order to reduce the amount of manual user inputs, the systems rely on context information. Usually, this context information is gathered unobtrusively by means of sensors that are integrated into some of the devices. As a simplification, we assume that the information that is gathered by the sensors is representing information about some of the devices in their vicinity. Given that the sensing range is often smaller than the communication range, we argue that this simplification is not overly restricting.

From a security perspective, the devices that are connected to each other at a particular point in time may span multiple domains that are administered independently. As a result, it is not safe to assume that all devices are equally trustworthy. Instead, the devices that are part of one administration domain may use their resources to change the behavior of the devices from another maliciously. As a consequence, it is necessary to ensure that critical decisions are based solely on valid context from trustworthy devices.

4.2.3 Example Scenario

To clarify the system model, consider the example scenario shown in Figure 4.2 that depicts a common research/university campus. To limit the access to the campus to legitimate persons, the whole area is enclosed by a fence and both, employees and visitors need to pass by a gatekeeper at the main entrance. Due to the size of the campus, there is a significant distance between the gatekeeper's location and the office buildings which makes it impossible to keep track of the visitors after they passed the gate. As a consequence, employees may have to pick up first-time visitors at the main entrance to ensure that they are not getting lost. In addition, the sheer size of the campus also makes it hard to ensure that illegitimate persons are not simply climbing over a fence.

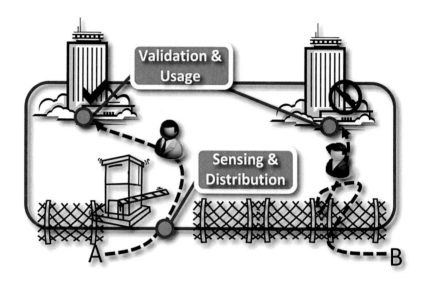

Figure 4.2: Example Scenario

To improve this situation, the access control performed by the gatekeeper can be revalidated at the entrance of the individual buildings by means of a pervasive application. When a person enters through the main gate, a sensor recognizes this and generates a corresponding piece of context information. Since the gatekeeper's office is not continuously connected to all building entrances, the sensor stores the context information on the mobile phone of the person. Once the person arrives at a building entrance, an actuator that is mounted to the entrance requests the context information from the mobile phone and it solely unlocks the entrance, if the person has been detected by the sensor at the gatekeeper (cf. A) which prevents illegitimate access (cf. B).

4.2.4 Requirements

From the peer-based system model presented previously and the desire to support the utilization of context information to automate security critical decisions, we can derive the requirements for context distribution as follows:

- **Decentralized provisioning:** As peer-based systems cannot provide guarantees about the availability of devices, the context information must be made available in a decentralized manner. More specifically, to ensure support for arbitrary disconnections, a particular piece of information must be stored on all devices to which it relates to.

- **Generic mechanisms:** The mechanisms used for context distribution should be generic with respect to the context information that shall be distributed. This ensures that they are applicable to a broad range of different applications.

- **Reliable security:** In order to enable the use of context information for security critical decisions, it is necessary to ensure that the information has actually been generated by a reliable source (authenticity). Furthermore, it is necessary to ensure that the information cannot be altered when stored on a device that is not trustworthy (integrity). Finally, in some cases it may be necessary to ensure that the information has been generated recently (freshness).

- **Configurable trust:** Since peer-based systems may span multiple administrative domains, it is not viable to rely on the context information generated from arbitrary devices. Instead, it is necessary to allow the configuration of trust in order to support the secure utilization of context generated in different domains.

- **Low resource usage:** Last but not least, in order to be applicable to resource-poor devices, the provisioning of the context information should not be a resource intensive task. Instead, the mechanisms for distribution should exhibit low resource utilization without endangering the security.

4.2.5 Context Distribution Framework

In the following, we describe our framework to support the secure distribution of context information. We will now first provide an overview of the basic framework and then describe the individual mechanisms and protocols. Then, we present some extensions to reduce the resource utilization. Finally, we briefly outline the prototypical implementation which is later evaluated in Chapter 8.

Figure 4.3: Framework Overview

Overview

To support the decentralized provisioning of context information while providing strong security, our framework decouples the tasks of sensing and distributing context from the task of validating it in space and time. To do this, the basic version of our framework relies on asymmetric cryptography. As we will show in the evaluation in Section 8.2, this approach is suitable for devices with limited resources such as SunSPOTs. However, to reduce the resource requirements even further, we provide a symmetric alternative.

As basis for asymmetric cryptography, we require that each device belonging to the same administrative domain is equipped with a key pair and a certificate that is signed by a common root certificate. Thus, the root certificate represents a single administrative domain and it can be used to identify the domain's trusted devices. Furthermore, we require that devices are identified by the fingerprint of their certificate which ensures that the identification is hard to compromise. The generation and distribution of the keys and certificates is done in an offline step that can be performed using standard tools such as OpenSSL.

On top of this setup, the basic variant of the framework differentiates three functionalities. As depicted in Figure 4.3, all functionalities rely on a key store that holds the keys and certificates described previously. The *generator* functionality is responsible for perceiving its environment by means of some sensor and for distributing the resulting context information. The *storage* functionality stores the context information provided by generators for later usage. The *validator* functionality retrieves and validates context information and depending on the result of the validation, it may initiate an action, e.g., by means of an actuator.

To perform the validation, the validator functionality must determine whether the context has been issued by a trusted generator component. To do this, the framework introduces a *distribution protocol* between the generator and the storage and a *validation protocol* between the storage and the

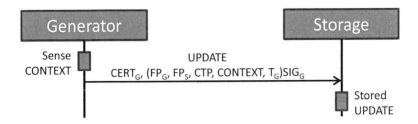

Figure 4.4: Distribution Protocol

validator. In the following, we provide a detailed description of these protocols. Thereafter, we describe an extension of the framework that replaces the distribution protocol with a symmetric variant.

Distribution Protocol

When the sensing unit of a generator perceives some new piece of information about a device, the generator stores the information in the storage of this device. To do this, the generator and the storage execute the distribution protocol. As depicted in Figure 4.4, the distribution protocol consists of a single update message that is initiated by the generator.

Besides the type of the context (CTP) and the actual information ($CONTEXT$), the update also contains the fingerprint identifiers of the generator device (FP_G) and the targeted storage device (FP_S). The context type and the actual information can be arbitrary byte sequences. The type itself is later on used in the validation protocol to request a particular piece of context. As stated previously, the identifiers refer to the fingerprints of the corresponding certificates. Thus, they provide a strong association between the generator and the storage. As we explain later on, this ensures that a piece of context information that has been generated for one device cannot be used by another. Finally, the update also contains a timestamp (T_G) of the generator as well as its certificate ($CERT_G$). During the validation, the timestamp is used to ensure the freshness of the information. The certificate is needed to enable the validation of arbitrary generators without knowing them a priori.

To ensure the authenticity and integrity of the update, the identifiers as well as the context type, information and time are signed using the private key of the generator. If necessary, this also allows the storage device to determine

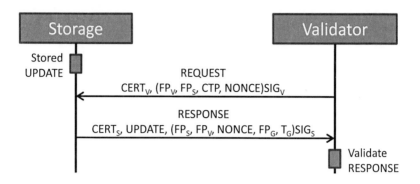

Figure 4.5: Validation Protocol

whether the context has been issued by a trustworthy generator. To do this, the storage would have to verify that $CERT_G$ has been signed by a trusted root certificate and that SIG_G is valid. However, this validation step at the storage is not required to enforce the security goals introduced earlier. Instead, the storage can simply store all updates as received.

Validation Protocol

If the validation is required, the validator is responsible for retrieving the context. As depicted in Figure 4.5, this requires a request and a response that (1) authenticates the storage and (2) transmits the verifiable information.

To achieve this, the request is composed of the context type (CTP) that shall be retrieved, the identifiers of the validator (FP_V) and the storage (FP_S), a nonce ($NONCE$) that is generated by the validator as well as its certificate ($CERT_V$). The identifiers, context type and the nonce are signed by the validator which can be used to enable the storage device to restrict requests to trusted validators. To do this, the storage verifies that $CERT_V$ is signed by a trusted root and that SIG_V is valid. However, just like the validation of the generator of an update, this is an optional step.

Similarly, the response to this request is composed of the certificate of the identifiers FP_V and FP_S and the nonce that was included in the request. Furthermore, it includes the identifier of the generator (FP_G) and the timestamp of the update (T_G) as well as the certificate of the storage ($CERT_S$) and the original update message. Finally, the message includes a signature for the identifiers, the nonce and the timestamp that is generated by the storage.

In order to validate the response, the validator first determines whether the nonces are identical, which verifies that the response matches the request. Thereafter, it determines whether the CTP in the update is as requested. Then, it determines whether FP_S, FP_G and T_G in the response are identical to the values in the update and whether the fingerprint of $CERT_S$ and $CERT_G$ are matching FP_S and FP_G. This ensures that the context was assigned to the right storage and is not yet expired. Finally, the validator verifies that the certificate of the generator is signed by a trusted root and that the signatures in the update (SIG_G) and the response (SIG_V) are valid.

Once this validation process has succeeded, the validator can accept the context. Thereby the process ensures that the storage device is authentic since it must be equipped with the private key for $CERT_S$ to create SIG_S and the response cannot be a replay as it includes FP_V and the correct nonce. Furthermore, the update message has not been changed during the transmission since the signature SIG_V also spans FP_G and T_G and they are identical to the update. Finally, the update has been issued for the storage device since it includes FP_S and it can be trusted since $CERT_G$ is signed by a trusted root and thus, the generator can be trusted.

In order to determine whether the context information itself is fresh (enough), the validator can use the timestamp of the generator (T_G). However, this requires that the clocks of the validator and the generator are (loosely) synchronized. This can either be achieved by an external time source such as a UTC or GPS receiver. Alternatively, trusted storage devices that regularly pass the generator and the validators can also perform the synchronization. To do this in a secure manner, it is possible to reuse the protocols described above. Thereby, the trusted storage device acts as a generator for the time and the actual context generator acts as a validator. To set the time on the context generator, the trusted storage device simply generates an update containing the current time that is used within the validation procedure performed by the generator.

Extensions

As indicated in the framework overview, it is possible to further reduce the resource utilization of the framework for generators by replacing the asymmetric signatures with their symmetric counterparts. For this to work, however, the validators and the generators must share the same *symmetric* key. If this can be achieved by means of key distribution, the protocols described above can be applied directly by removing $CERT_G$ from the update and by replacing SIG_G with a symmetric signature based on the shared key.

However, besides increasing the effort for key distribution, the main drawback of this approach is a loss in flexibility when context shall be used across different administrative domains. In the asymmetric case, it is possible to define unidirectional trust-relations. To do this, a validator can simply be configured to trust the generators of a certain (set of) domain(s). In the symmetric case, this is not possible as the distribution of the key would result in a symmetric trust-relationship since every validator could forge the values of the generator.

To mitigate this problem, our framework introduces so-called generator bridges or simply *bridges*. The bridges are responsible for replacing the symmetric signatures with asymmetric ones. To do this, they request the context information from the storage, they validate the symmetric signature and they create a corresponding update message. This requires them to be configured with the symmetric key of the generator and an asymmetric key pair that shall represent the generator.

Implementation

The framework has been implemented as an extension to BASE [BSGR03], our communication middleware for peer-based pervasive systems. We have implemented individual services for symmetric and asymmetric generators, storages, validators and bridges. These services provide interfaces to distribute arbitrary context information that can be used in different applications. Towards this end, the generator services must be extended with a sensing unit that creates the context information. The validators must be extended with an actuation unit that requests the context information. In addition to these services, we have implemented a service to distribute the root certificates within an administration domain. Although not being secure, in general, this service enables the user to detect new root certificates and to decide whether they want to trust them. In addition, it could be used to distribute certificate revocation lists.

All services share a common key store functionality which is used to configure the device and its trust-relations. Thus, besides from storing the certificate and key of a device, the key store also stores trustworthy and untrusted (but discovered) certificates. To represent these certificates, we rely on the X.509

standard [CSF$^+$08]. In order to associate the fingerprints of the certificates with devices, we use them as BASE's system identifier.

To realize the cryptographic algorithms, we reuse the implementations of the J2ME version of Bouncycastle library [The]. This allows the utilization of RSA and ECC as asymmetric methods. Both can be used at the same time by different generators or administrative domains. For symmetric authentication, we rely on HMAC [KBC97] using the SHA-1 hash algorithm. Of course, other types could easily be added, so our framework does not depend on a particular cryptographic algorithm.

Since Bouncycastle is applicable to all devices that provide a Java virtual machine with J2ME CLDC support, the library itself is not optimized for a particular type of device. Thus, to get realistic estimations for the overhead of the framework, we are using an optimized implementation for SunSPOTs. This implementation makes use of the SunSPOT SSL library which provides a fast 160-bits ECC implementation using SECP160r1. The resulting encryption strength is comparable to an RSA key size of 1024 bits. However, it is noteworthy that the optimized version of our prototype can interact with non-optimized versions without modification.

4.3 Conclusion

Providing adequate support for context acquisition and management is a non-trivial task that complicates the development of ubiquitous applications, but is required since context information is vital for automation. Here, we presented a peer-based alternative to centralized context management which overcomes privacy issues by supporting a fine-granular device- and thus, user-dependent definition of sharing policies. Especially in cases where automated decision may have security implications, ensuring the validity of context information is unavoidable. So, we have additionally derived the requirements on secure context distribution and usage in peer-based systems as well as developed a generic framework to satisfy them. The framework can achieve a high level of security that keeps up with current Internet standards while being applicable to many scenarios.

Although, our current implementation enables a fine-granular protection of the user's context, the actual policy specification must be done statically upfront. In Chapter 7, we describe a mechanism that eases this process for the user and automates the specification of a privacy policy.

Both approaches are targeting resource-constrained, Java-based devices like SunSPOTs which allow them to be integrated into everyday objects. This integration is a first step towards the realization of the pervasive computing vision. After the development of these approaches, they were integrated into the PECES middleware as part of the PECES European project. Using the peer-based context management, they form the basis to allow the secure adaptation with role assignment to dynamically form smart spaces and to enable their interaction across insecure networks such as the Internet.

5 Secure Adaptation with Role Assignment

The chapter *Secure Adaptation with Role Assignment* is focused on the concept of role assignment. While the previous chapter described how context information can be securely distributed in peer-based environments, this chapter presents role assignment as the next logical step for pervasive environments. Secure role assignment requires secure context management, since roles and adaptation decisions are often based on context information. Additionally, roles are often used to restrict the environment, i.e., devices are not always perceived as peers, but are used according to their assigned role(s). Going further into this direction, roles can create so-called *smart spaces* or *smart environments* that may interact with each other, but can also act independently, as isolated islands. Here, we describe our approach for secure adaptation with role assignment which is another step towards environments that realize the vision of pervasive computing.

5.1 Preliminaries

As described previously, one of the main goals of pervasive computing is to provide the user with seamless and distraction-free task support. This task support is realized by pervasive applications that are running on devices integrated into everyday objects. Using sensors, they are able to perceive information about their physical context and using actuators, they may manipulate parts of it. Due to their integration, the devices are heterogeneous and may exhibit mobility. These factors lead to a dynamic environment. Because of this, applications need to adapt to the environment continuously. If the environment changes frequently, a manual adaptation by the user is not feasible as this might cause significant distraction. Therefore, it is necessary to automate the adaptation. Implementing this automation at the application layer is a complicated and error-prone process and leads to a considerable development overhead.

To ease application development, existing middleware systems for pervasive computing can provide a diverse set of supportive mechanisms. While at the lowest level, they can provide basic networking functionality, service abstractions or component frameworks, while at higher levels, they may provide intelligent automation, for example, to adapt applications to user preferences or to the available devices. Intuitively, the resource utilization of the adaptation and many other of these mechanisms provided by the middleware is tightly tied to the number of devices that must be considered. As an example at the networking level, consider a mediator-based discovery scheme in which a central device collects all device information. Such a scheme may only work effectively in scenarios with a limited number of devices. At the automation level, the same holds true. For example, to automatically adapt a distributed application, it is often necessary to compute possible configurations. As the number of possible configurations increases with the number of devices, this kind of automation is hard to apply to large scale systems.

Since distant objects are often less relevant to an application than objects in the proximity, middleware systems typically exploit locality to improve performance. To do this, they introduce logical boundaries on the environment that reduce the number of devices. Although, the idea of exploiting locality is suitable in many scenarios, there are several cases in which applications may need to interact with distant devices. Some examples are scenarios that require access to resources in a remote smart environment or scenarios that require the remote collaboration of users in two separate smart environments.

Here, we show how this problem can be avoided by means of using role assignment for environment configuration at the middleware layer. An application can then specify its adaptation requirements to the middleware. The middleware automates the adaptation decisions and may even execute the resulting changes. Additionally, in many application scenarios, adaptation decisions can have critical security implications. Consider an application for document editing that automatically migrates its output from the small screen of the user's mobile phone to a larger screen available in the environment. If the screen has been set-up by a malicious person, it may be possible to copy the displayed documents. This problem is amplified, if a service in a remote environment is mediated over the Internet. As a result, it is necessary to consider security constraints when designing a middleware that automates adaptation.

In this chapter, we present generic role assignment and extend it to support security constraints. This combination allows us to perform secure adaptations with role assignment. We present the following contributions: We first derive the requirements on environment configuration and thereafter, we describe how role assignment can be used as its basis. Then, we define a simple yet flexible model to capture the trust relationships between different devices. On the basis of this, we extend role assignment with special rules to model security requirements. Additionally, we discuss the necessary changes to enable their automatic enforcement at runtime. As validation of our contributions, we describe a prototypical implementation of a secure role assignment system and we describe several system services that we built on top of it.

5.2 Requirements

The requirements presented here are motivated from our primary goal for secure adaptation with role assignment which is the ability to use its resulting role assignments as basis to develop security critical pervasive computing applications. The first step to achieve this is the identification of a set of devices of a pervasive computing system that may interact with each other. Intuitively, due to the dynamics of the underlying systems, the identification of these devices must be done continuously at runtime. From this step and our security goal, we can derive the following requirements on solutions that identify the set and allow to use it with security critical pervasive applications.

- **Configurable:** In environment configuration, the maximal set of devices is usually defined technically by means of connectivity. However, in order to maximize the performance, environment configuration typically strives for determining a minimum set. Yet, in many cases it is not feasible to clearly define the minimal set without running the risk of excluding devices that may be relevant for an application, a suitable definition may often be scenario-specific. Additionally, to achieve the goal of secure role assignment, it is necessary to enable the developer to specify security requirements at different levels of abstraction. For example, a developer might want to directly limit role assignment to a set of devices that is known at development time. For other applications, a developer might want to perform role assignment only with the set of devices that are trustworthy from a user's perspective. As a consequence, a generic solution for environment configuration should be configurable in order to support the definition of effective boundaries in a scenario-specific way. Furthermore, since not all adaptation decisions must be secured, the security should be optional.

- **Composable:** In order to avoid the introduction of artificial boundaries, environment configuration should support the on-demand extension of existing environments. However, to avert side-effects between different applications and to allow the independent development of various definitions for the execution environment, the extension of the environment must be done in a controlled manner. To do this, environment configuration should support the composition of new environments by composing them from existing ones.

- **Flexible:** Since distant objects are often less relevant to an application than objects in the proximity, existing middleware systems are exploiting locality to define the boundaries. Thereby, they consider a single characteristic of the context of a device such as a geographic location or physical proximity. Although, this approach has been proposed several times, it often does not result in minimal sets. In many scenarios, characteristics such as the device owner, for example, can be used more easily and result in smaller sets. Thus, instead of being fixed to a single context characteristic such as location, environment configuration should support the flexible definition of boundaries on various context characteristics.

- **Light-weight:** The devices in the pervasive computing domain are often heterogeneous and may include resource-constrained devices like sensors. To be able to use such devices, secure adaptation with role assignment should be light-weight. In cases where security is not needed, its security mechanisms should not introduce additional costs. Furthermore, in order to support resource-poor devices, the mechanisms that are needed for configuration should exhibit a small size and if security is required, the resulting overheads should not introduce high performance penalties.

- **Secure:** Since the decisions made during role assignment may have critical security implications, the security provided by role assignment must be high. Despite the fact that devices can be resource-constrained, malicious persons may have a significant amount of resources at their disposal. This is especially true, if role assignment is performed across an insecure network such as the Internet. Consequently, the concepts used to secure role assignment should allow the use of cryptographic methods that exhibit Internet-level strength.

5.3 Approach

To provide a solution to environment configuration that fulfills the requirements described previously, we base our solution on the idea of role assignment. As a consequence, we first describe our overall idea of role assignment before we discuss how it can be applied to the problem of environment configuration. We then extend our work with security concepts and describe the individual security aspects in detail.

5.3.1 Generic Role Assignment

Building on the work of [HHM09], the basis for generic role assignment is a set of devices that can communicate with each other. We assume that each device has some a priori knowledge about its context and that it is able to perceive parts of its context at runtime. Given that a lot of context such as the device type and owner for example are usually static and that more dynamic context such as the device's location can often be acquired automatically by means of built-in sensors or by retrieving sensor values from other devices, this assumption can be fulfilled by most mobile devices today. Furthermore, we assume that the context of a device is stored locally so that it can be accessed when needed.

Based on these assumptions, generic role assignment uses the device's context to assign roles. A *role* is essentially a tag that can be assigned to one or more devices. By definition, a role is assigned to any device as long as there are no further constraints that limit the assignment. To enable the automated computation of an assignment that reflects a particular goal, we introduce *rules*. Rules define contextual constraints on the assignment of roles to devices.

In [HHM09], Haroon et al. identified 4 different classes of rules to support a broad range of configuration tasks. However, for environment configuration, we only require two classes of rules, which we call *filter rule* and *reference rule*. A filter rule simply constraints the set of devices to a set of devices that exhibits a particular context. An example for such a filter rule is to demand that all devices should be at a certain location. In contrast, a reference rule references other role assignments. As an example for such a reference consider a rule that demands that a device must exhibit a particular role. Thus, by using reference rules, it is possible to assign roles hierarchically. The set of roles together with their corresponding rules form a role specification. To express complex logic, a single role may be constrained using several rules that are combined using the logical AND and OR operators. The logical NOT operator is not supported as this can easily lead to sets that require the evaluation of all globally connected devices. In practice, we did not find this to be problematic since it is usually possible to avoid NOT operators by an explicit enumeration of filters.

Given that the necessary contextual information is known to each device, we can automatically assign roles to the devices whose context satisfies the constraints specified by their rules. Alternatively, we may also empower a user to manually assign roles to support cases where the necessary context is not available or where automation is not desirable. However, here, we focus on the automatic assignment, exclusively.

It is worth noting that a similar concept has also been proposed to configure sensor networks [FR05] and distributed robot systems [INPS03]. However, the role specification and algorithms used in these works are specific to monitoring tasks and distributed robot coordination. As a consequence, the overall architecture and role specification language differ significantly. For example, the approach taken in [FR05] focuses primarily on network-related metrics whereas [INPS03] applies utility functions to achieve a targeted coverage.

5.3.2 Adaptive Environment Role Assignment

To use the generic role assignment for secure adaptation, i.e., for environment configuration, we can use role *specifications* to define the boundaries. The actual assignment of a single role can then be used to define the set of devices. Thereby, we may reason about roles from the perspective of the device, i.e., whether the device has a certain role, or from the perspective of the overall system, i.e., which set of devices has a certain role. Thus, we can identify whether a particular device belongs to the environment and we can identify the total set of devices that form the environment.

Figure 5.1 shows an example for this. To specify the typical boundaries of a smart space, a developer can create a role specification that assigns Role A to all devices whose location is known to be inside Home A. To do this, the developer creates a filter rule for the location and attaches it to Role A. After the assignment, the devices within the home can be identified by the role. Intuitively, in order to cope with changes, the assignment process must be performed at regular intervals. Similarly, in order to specify the boundaries on the basis of device ownership, a developer can specify a filter rule that constraints the set of devices to a particular person (Role B). In order to combine these sets of devices, two reference rules can be used to reference the roles A and B. Using Boolean operators it is possible to further restrict the set of devices, e.g., to only select mobile ones. As we discuss later on, the resulting role assignments can then be used independently from their definition to optimize middleware functions.

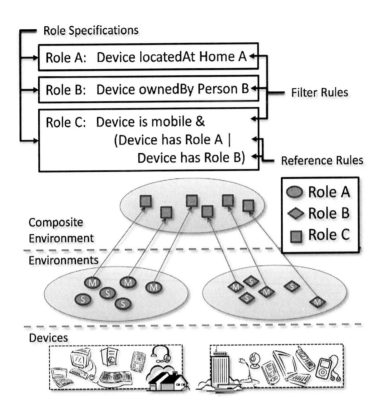

Figure 5.1: Using Role Assignment for Environment Configuration.

5.3.3 Secure Role Assignment

The basic idea of the secure role assignment is to secure the input data that is used during role assignment. Since generic role assignment introduces two classes of rules, this affects two types of data. For filter rules, it is necessary to ensure that the context used during their evaluation corresponds to the actual situation. From a systems perspective[1], this can be achieved by

---

[1]We are aware of the fact that there are other possibilities. For example, one might argue that a correspondency is given, if n arbitrary sensors make similar observations. However, such definitions are orthogonal to our approach.

ensuring that the situation has been observed by a trustworthy sensor[2] and that the observation has not been altered. Furthermore, since the context may change over time, it may also be necessary to ensure that the observation has been made recently. For reference rules, it is necessary to ensure that the roles used during reference resolution have been assigned properly. To do this, it is necessary to ensure that the role has been assigned by the device responsible for a particular role specification and that the role has not been altered. As role assignment is a dynamic process, it may also be necessary to ensure that the role is not outdated. Thus, we need to secure the authenticity and integrity of context and roles and optionally, we also need to ensure their freshness.

As a first step, it is necessary to define the set of trustworthy devices. To do this, we introduce a simple trust model that is based on certificate hierarchies. In the model, a certificate is attached to every device. The certificates are used to identify devices and capture the devices' memberships in different administrative domains. As a second step, we then extend the role specification with an additional class of so-called security rules which define the set of devices or domains regarded as trustworthy. In order to enable user-specific definitions of trust, we introduce trust-levels that can be defined for each device. The levels can be referenced in an abstract manner within the security rules. At runtime, the levels are then automatically resolved into the proper set of device-specific certificates. Due to the fact that the security rules cause additional effort during the role assignment process, the rules can be attached to individual filter or reference rules. Besides from reducing the overhead, this approach also increases the configurability. As a third step, we then ensure the enforcement of the security rules during the evaluation of the corresponding filter and reference rules which realizes the design goal of security.

5.3.4 Trust Model

Defining the set of trustworthy devices, trust can be modeled in many different ways [LKPW09, KNS05, Ser04]. For our approach, we chose to base our trust model on the widely used concept of certificate hierarchies [CSF+08] depicted in Figure 5.2. The reason for this is twofold. First, certificate hierarchies exhibit both, scalability at deployment as well as at runtime. By means of hierarchical relationships, devices can be grouped into an arbitrary number of administration domains. Furthermore, it is possible to add new

---

[2]If certain facts are not observed directly but modeled by a human (e.g., device ownership, etc.), the modeling person must be trustworthy.

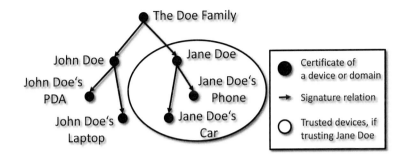

Figure 5.2: Certificate Hierarchy and Trust Model Example

devices to established domains at any point in time (i.e., by signing a device's certificate with the corresponding domain certificate). At runtime, it is then possible to automatically detect and verify a device's membership in a decentralized manner (i.e., by validating the signatures of a known sub-tree). Second, as a side-effect of using certificates, it is possible to generate a unique, cryptographically strong device identifier (e.g., by using the certificate's fingerprint as device id).

Using the certificate hierarchies, we enable the user to assign different levels of trust to one or more certificates. An example for this is depicted in Figure 5.2. If the certificate represents an administrative domain, intuitively, the trust recursively expands to all devices that it contains. For example, in Figure 5.2, by putting a particular level of trust in the certificate that represents Jane Doe, the trust expands to all of Jane Doe's devices. In order to reduce the modeling effort, we order the trust levels and assume transitivity such that a lower level includes the higher levels. Consequently, the two extremes are full trust and no trust. Between those two levels, we allow an arbitrary number of additional levels with an application-defined meaning. Additionally, applications can modify the trust level of certificates based on their needs.

5.3.5 Security Rules

To secure the input data that is used during role assignment, we extend the role specification by introducing a new class of rules, so-called *security rules*. Security rules enable the specification of two types of security requirements. They allow the specification of a minimum amount of trust that is required

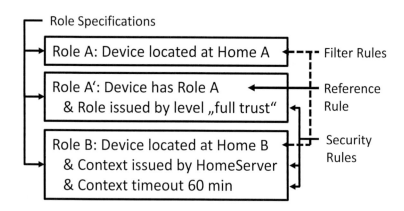

Figure 5.3: Role Specification with Security Rules Example

to consider a data source during role assignment. This can be done either directly by referencing devices or administration domains by the means of their certificates. Alternatively, it is possible to indirectly reference devices by requiring a particular trust level. Second and in addition to trust, the security rules enable the specification of a maximum age of data.

The security rules can then be assigned to filter and reference rules in a fine-granular manner. An example for the resulting role specifications is depicted in Figure 5.3. The figure shows three role specifications. The first one assigns a role *Role A* to a device whose location is at *Home A*. The second specification references *Role A* in the previous specification, but in addition it requires that the role ought to be assigned by a device that is classified as *full trust*. Consequently, this role will only be applied to devices that are equipped with a certificate that exhibits the trust level *full trust*. Note that due to the trust model, this may apply to both, devices that have been identified as such directly as well as devices that exhibit a certificate whose signatures are rooted in a *full trust* certificate. The third example specification defines *Role B* which is only assigned to devices that are located at *Home B*. Using security rules, the distribution of this role is restricted to devices whose location has been observed by a device called *HomeServer* and this observation has been made at most 60 minutes ago.

5.3.6 Security Enforcement

After having defined the trust model and the security rules, the third and final step is to ensure the security enforcement during role assignment. Due to the fact that the security rules can be added to both, filter rules and reference rules, it is necessary to enable the enforcement for context as well as roles. In the following, we briefly describe how the enforcement can be realized for each type of data.

Context

To enable the enforcement with respect to context we must be able to ensure the authenticity of the source. Furthermore, we must be able to ensure the integrity of the context and we must be able to determine its age. To do this, we apply the *generator*, *storage* and *validator* principle that we developed in Section 4.2 in the previous chapter. For the sake of brevity, we briefly discuss the problem mapping in the following and outline the basic idea. For our application scenario, *generators* are mapped to devices that gather context by means of their built-in sensors. *Storages* are mapped to devices that store this context and make it accessible for role assignment[3]. *Validators* are mapped to devices that evaluate role specifications and perform the role assignment. Using the update and validation protocols described in Section 4.2.5, validators can verify the authenticity, integrity and freshness of the context gathered by generators, even if the storage device is malicious. To do this, the protocols utilize cryptographic signatures as well as some additional meta information that is attached to the context. Note that in order to support resource-constrained devices, the protocols do not require asymmetric cryptography on all devices. Instead, they can also apply hash-based message authentication codes as a light-weight replacement on resource-poor devices.

By applying this mapping, validators – that is devices evaluating a role specification – can directly validate the authenticity, integrity and freshness of the context supplied by the (storage) devices which they test. They must compare the requirements defined in the role specification with the context's meta information and they must validate the cryptographic signatures. Due to the use of certificate hierarchies, this might require the additional exchange of the certificate chain of the generator. Towards this end, the generator has to be modified in such a way that it attaches the chain as part

---

[3]Note that generators and storages can be represented by the same device.

of the update protocol – which transmits context from the generator to the storage.

Roles

To enforce the security requirements with respect to roles, there are two possible options. First, it is possible to utilize the principles applied to context analogously. To do this, assigned roles must be extended with meta information by the source device that assigns a role to a target device. Just like with context, this meta information must include a time stamp, the source and the target device identifiers as well as the certificate chain of the source device. The result can then be protected against manipulation using a cryptographic signature before it is transferred to the target device. When a reference rule is extended with a security rule, any device can then validate the role assignment by the following process. If the security role requires a certain freshness, the age of the assignment is validated by checking the time stamp. Now, it is necessary to validate whether the source device exhibits (at least) the required trust level. So, the source identifier and the identifiers contained in its certificate chain must be matched against the certificates that exhibit (at least) the required trust level. If this is the case, the signatures along the certificate chain as well as the signature of the role need to be validated. As an alternative, it is also possible to enforce the security requirements by retrieving the role and the meta data directly from the source device through a secure connection. This alleviates the need to cryptographically sign the role. To establish such a connection, it is possible to use the devices' certificates to guarantee authenticity and to generate a shared symmetric key which can then be used to guarantee integrity as well as secrecy.

Both approaches have advantages and disadvantages. The main advantage of the first possibility is that it does not require a direct connection between the source device that assigns a role and the device that aims at validating the role. However, in order to support validation, it is either necessary to use comparatively heavyweight asymmetric cryptography or to have a shared symmetric key which must be distributed somehow. For the former, the resulting overhead can be high, especially if many roles must be validated or if roles need to be validated periodically. In such cases, it is more efficient to opt for a secure connection. The additional effort for connection establishment can then be easily amortized over time. Since both approaches can be beneficial, depending on their usage, we propose to apply both of them on a case-by-case basis.

5.4 Implementation

To validate our approach, we have implemented a prototypical role assignment system and extended it with the security related concepts and mechanisms described previously. Furthermore, we have used it to develop a number of additional security critical middleware services. The resulting implementation is available as open source under BSD license[4]. In the following, we first describe the architectural components. Thereafter, we describe how they interact. Finally, we describe a number of middleware services that we have built on top of our system for secure adaptation with role assignment.

5.4.1 Architecture

Similar to the previous chapter on context management, we rely on BASE [HBS03] to enable communication between devices. BASE provides the basic communication functionality such as support for device discovery and interaction. On top of that, BASE provides a basic service model that we use to implement the remaining layers of the role assignment system. Thereby, every building block is implemented as a well-known service that can be accessed locally and remotely.

To automate role assignment, the system needs to be able to automatically capture context information. Due to the differences in sensor APIs for various devices, the acquisition must usually be done in a device-dependent manner. Additionally, the context management layer is responsible for abstracting from the details of gathering context information by providing a uniform query interface. As described in Section 4.1, we are using RDF [Wora] to represent context information. This enables data modeling and reasoning on the basis of standard ontology languages such as OWL. OWL ontologies are often used in pervasive computing environments due to their flexibility and expressiveness [CFJ03, WZGP04, BCQ$^+$07]. In order to query the RDF data, we use SPARQL [Worb] basic graph matching patterns which we extend with non-standard geo-spatial extensions for range and nearest-neighbor queries. This allows us to express location-based queries which are often useful for environment configuration. Consequently, filter rules are formulated as SPARQL queries whose successful evaluation determines whether a device matches the filter. In order to support context provisioning on resource-poor devices, we have implemented two alternative context services for different classes of devices. On resource-rich devices, we use JENA [Apa]

---

[4]Documentation and code are accessible via http://peces.googlecode.com.

and ARQ to store context and to evaluate queries. On resource-poor devices, such as mobile phones or SunSPOTs, we use a custom implementation that stores all context information in-memory and implements a large subset of the SPARQL language with limited reasoning capabilities over a set of statically compiled ontologies.

On top, the generic role assignment layer provides the functionality to define role specifications using roles and rules. Once a role specification is passed to the role assignment layer, it can automatically perform the assignment using context information. To do this, the layer provides an assignment service that computes an assignment. Once the assignment has been computed, the roles need to be distributed to the devices. This enables them to determine whether they exhibit a certain role. To perform this distribution in an application-independent manner, the role assignment layer includes a notification service which is notified by the assignment service whenever a local assignment changes. Note that the assignment service is not needed by each device. Instead, it is only necessary on those devices that are actually computing an assignment. Thus, to minimize the resource consumption, it is possible to deploy only the notification service.

At the service layer, other services and applications may use the role assignments to optimize their mechanisms. Thereby, they can use the local notification service to react to changes of roles. Alternatively, they can query the assignment service in order to retrieve the current assignment. The former reflects the per device view, the latter reflects the system view.

In summary and as pictured in Figure 5.4, the five main layers are communication, security, context management, role assignment and services that use the assignment as environment definition. Communication is handled by means of a BASE id (unique to each device) which hides the technology specific communication address (e.g., MAC or IP) from the application developer. For the context management, we implemented a context storage that stores arbitrary context in the form of RDF that can be structured using OWL ontologies and queried using SPARQL queries.

In order to implement the security concepts described in Section 5.3, we extend the basic architecture with a number of additional components. The resulting architecture is also depicted in Figure 5.4. The components of the generic role assignment are marked in black whereas the security extensions are shaded gray.

At the communication layer, we extend the architecture with two additional BASE plugins that provide secure connections using symmetric cryptography (via AES and HMAC) and enable different variants of the Diffie-Hellman

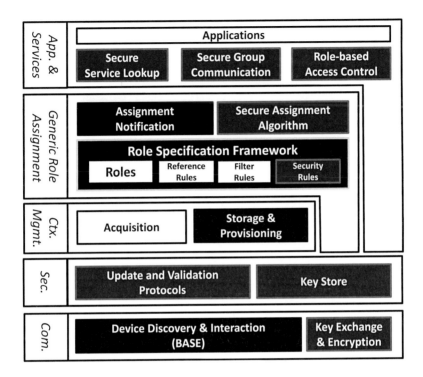

Figure 5.4: Secure Role Assignment System Architecture

key exchange (i.e., DH and ECDH). To implement the trust model and to manage pre-shared symmetric as well as asymmetric keys and certificates (i.e., RSA and ECC), we add a key store component. Besides from managing pre-deployed keys and certificates, the key store is also able to cache symmetric keys (and verified certificate chains) that are established (and verified) using the key exchange plug-ins. Furthermore, we add a component that is capable of signing and validating context information and roles using the update and validation protocols described in Section 4.2. To define security requirements, we extend the role specification framework with the security rules described in Section 5.3.5.

5.4.2 Interaction

To clarify the architecture, we describe the runtime interaction of its components in the following. As explained earlier, each device is equipped with an instance of BASE and the additional services that form the role assignment system. In order to support secure role assignment, each device must be configured with an asymmetric key pair as well as the chain of certificates that define its membership in different domains. Optionally, it may also be equipped with a number of pre-shared keys. In addition, if a device wants to start secure role assignments (i.e., it provides the assignment service), it also needs to know the certificates of domains that are trustworthy for the application. These can either be specified directly as part of a role specification, or they can be stored in the key store with their associated trust level - which is then resolved at runtime. Intuitively, this trust configuration does not have to be performed by the developer but could also be done by an administrator or an advanced user.

As explained earlier, each device is equipped with an instance of BASE and the additional services that form the role assignment system. To configure an environment or an application, a middleware service may start a role specification by sending it to a device equipped with an assignment service. Since multiple role specifications may use the same role identifiers, the role assignment service first creates a globally unique id for the specification. This enables the unique identification of individual roles which is required to reference a particular role. To do this, the role assignment service concatenates the BASE device id with a locally unique id.

Once a role specification is injected into the assignment service, the algorithm first interprets the security requirements of the specification. If a filter rule is associated with a security rule, the query evaluation for the filter rule cannot be executed on the context storage of the remote device – as the remote device could easily send an arbitrary response. Instead, it must be done locally on the device hosting the assignment service and it should only be done using context from a trustworthy source. In order to do that in an efficient manner, the assignment service creates a list of all SPARQL queries that represent the filter rules and sends the query to the remote device. Using the query, the context storage of the remote device determines and transmits the subset of RDF triples that is required to produce the query result. Once the triples are received, the assignment service validates them as described in Section 5.3.6. Thereafter, it locally executes the query on the subset of triples that meet the security requirements and computes the (possible) assignment. Although, this approach requires a duplicate query execution –

on the remote device as well as on the device hosting the assignment service – the filtering of RDF triples can often significantly reduce the amount of communication, especially in cases where devices store a lot of context. In addition, the query for filter rules are usually batched and send as one query to all connected devices. This reduces the amount of communication even further.

If a reference rule is associated with a security rule, the assignment service first determines the device responsible for the assignment by forwarding the specification to the assignment service that is executing the referenced role specification. If a role contains multiple references, the specification is forwarded to each referenced assignment service. The assignment service that receives the specification will then execute it locally. Thereby, it considers only those reference rules that reference local assignments. The other rules are simply ignored. Using the key store, it first checks whether the two devices already share a symmetric key. If this is not the case, the key exchange plug-in is used to establish a symmetric key. Using either the cached or the newly established key, the device then creates a secure connection to the device responsible for the assignment. Using the secure connection, the assignment service can then retrieve roles and validate meta information directly. In the end, a list of candidate assignments is returned to the original assignment component. There, the candidate assignments are transformed into final assignments. To do this, the assignment component may have to intersect or unify the candidate sets in order to compute the result in cases where multiple references are concatenated using a conjunction or a disjunction.

Once the role assignment has been computed, the role assignment service distributes the roles by informing the necessary devices through their notification component. Depending on the usage of the roles, this may either entail the creation of a signature – in cases where the role must be validated without establishing a secure connection – or it may entail the establishment of a secure connection to the receiving device. After accepting the role, the notification component on the receiving device can then notify applications that have registered locally for changes to role assignments.

An example for this process is depicted in Figure 5.5. The figure shows 7 devices that execute two role specifications. The first role specification defines two environments using the roles A and B. Both roles solely rely on filter rules in order to define the sets of devices. In order to keep the figure simple, we refrain from using SPARQL syntax, instead we simply assume that role A requires context A and role B requires context B. Once the role specification is started at device 6, the device assigns a unique id,

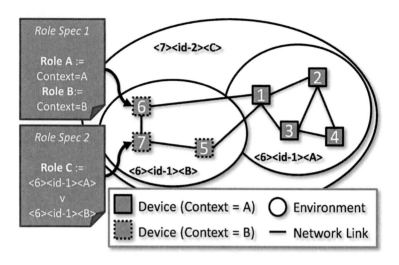

Figure 5.5: Generic Role Assignment Example

i.e. <6><id-1>. Thus, the roles can be identified by concatenating the role specification id with the role name, i.e. <6><id-1><A> or <6><id-1><B>. Since there are only filter rules, the assignment component queries the context of the connected devices and computes the assignment according to the rules. Finally, the assignment component notifies all devices that received a particular role.

The second role specification in the example refers to the first specification to define an environment using role C that consists of all devices that have role A or B. When the role specification is started at device 7, the unique id is generated and the role specification is analyzed. Since the role specification contains reference rules, the role specification is forwarded to the devices that are managing the referenced specification. In this example, this is done by device 6. To determine the managing device, the device 7 can simply use the BASE id that is embedded in the reference. Device 6 then computes the candidate set consisting of devices with role A and role B and returns it to device 7 which performs the final assignment. In this example, the candidate set and the final set are identical. However, if several specifications on multiple devices are referenced, it may be impossible to determine the set locally on the referenced devices. Once the set has been computed, device 7 notifies all relevant devices.

5.4.3 Integration

To validate the architecture of the role assignment system with respect to its interfaces, we modified the BASE service registry so that it benefits from the environment configuration. In addition, we have implemented a BASE communication plug-in that provides (optionally secure) environment-based communication. On top of that, the secure assignment of roles allows to establish role-based access control. In the following, we briefly outline the implementation.

To enable the spontaneous interaction of devices, BASE not only supports device discovery and interaction but it also provides a simple service abstraction. In order to find local and remote services, BASE provides a service registry. To support the dynamics of pervasive systems, the BASE service registry uses a reactive federation scheme. Each BASE-enabled device is equipped with a local registry that can be accessed locally as well as remotely. In order to export a service, an application simply calls an export function on the local registry which stores the associated service information. To search for available services, an application can call a search function locally. Internally, the search is then automatically distributed across all devices in order to return the complete set of services.

To improve the efficiency of the federation scheme, we have extended the registry to support the search within a particular environment. To do this, an application developer can define an environment using a role specification. Later on, the developer can search within the environment by sending a query and an associated globally unique role identifier to the local registry. Internally, the registry will then first contact the assignment service to retrieve the devices that exhibit the role and later on, it will only forward the queries to these devices. Thus, we speed up the search by minimizing the set of devices.

Using the role-based service registry, the role assignment can be secured by the application developer using security rules. Instead of using a secure transfer, they are signed by the assigning device. Thus, when a service search is executed, the devices that should retrieve the search query can be evaluated in a scalable, decentralized manner, without requiring interaction with the device that assigned the roles.

In addition to this, we have implemented a BASE communication plug-in that provides secure environment-based communication. Similar to the service registry, the communication plug-in restricts the distribution of a particular message to an environment that is defined by a role assignment. To

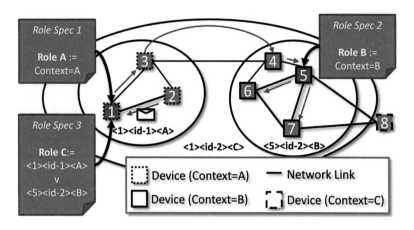

Figure 5.6: Role-based Communication

distribute the load of message forwarding, the plug-in uses the hierarchy that is created by reference rules for distribution. When a device receives a role, it may use the role to join a group communication channel using the BASE plug-in. If a message must be transmitted, the plug-in simply forwards the message to the device that performs the assignment. This device then forwards it to other devices, either directly – if it has performed the assignment – or indirectly – if it uses another device to compute candidate sets. To use this service in a secure manner, we added optional encryption using a group key. A developer can define security requirements on the group by defining a role with security rules. The role assignment system then automatically enforces them and ensures that only appropriate devices will receive the role. Before the roles are distributed, we first create a symmetric group key which we then distribute together with the role. To avoid overhearing, the role is transmitted to each device using a pair-wise encrypted channel. If devices leave the group, the role is updated. Once a role is received or updated, the new key is used for encryption. A group key substitution can therefore be performed with a role update. This ensures that only group members are actually able to participate in the communication.

An example for this is depicted in Figure 5.6. If Device 2 sends a message using the channel defined by Role C, it forwards the message to Device 1, since this device is responsible for performing the assignment. Device 1, in turn, uses Device 5 to compute parts of the assignment and thus, it forwards the message to this device. Furthermore, Device 1 distributes the message

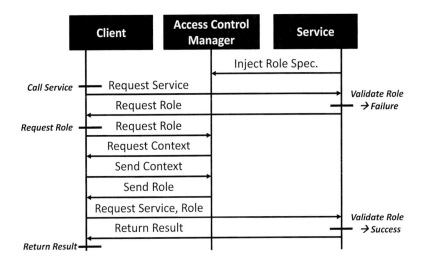

Figure 5.7: Role-based Access Control Example

to all devices with the Role A, since it has performed the assignment for this role. If the message arrives at Device 5, the device distributes the message to all devices with Role B, since it is responsible for assigning this role.

When secure roles are used, it is possible to develop additional services such as a role-based access control service. Here, we apply a similar approach as for the role-based service registry. Instead of using asymmetric signatures, we use HMAC with a symmetric key. The resulting interaction is depicted in Figure 5.7. To secure a service with role-based access control, the developer first specifies roles that represent a client's possible access rights. To ensure that the roles are assigned properly, the developer secures them with security rules.

When the service is started, the system injects the role specification into an assignment algorithm – either on the local device or a trustworthy device in the vicinity. To ensure that the role specification is not altered, this is done via a secure connection which will establish a key between the device hosting the service and the device performing access control. When a client attempts to access the service, the service first determines whether the client request contains the necessary role. If the request does not contain this role, the system generates an exception which is returned to the client. The exception notifies the client that the service requires a particular role that is assigned by a particular device responsible for access control. The role's id contains the BASE device id of the responsible access control manager. In order to get this role, the client contacts the access control manager and requests it. Then the access control manager performs the normal sequence of secure role assignment with this device. This involves sending the query for filter rules, resolving references, validating signatures, etc. Once this process has completed, the access control manager signs the roles using HMAC and the symmetric key of the device that hosts the service. Then it forwards the role to the client. Thereafter, the client attaches the roles and repeats the request. The service can then validate the role by validating the HMAC using the key shared with the access control manager. If the validation succeeds, the service is executed and the result is returned. For subsequent calls, the client simply reattaches the role to the request as long as it is fresh enough. Once the role is expired, the procedure repeats from the beginning. Although, this might look like a fairly complicated procedure, our implementation of role-based access control hides most of the details in automatically generated stubs and skeletons. The only interactions that are visible to the client developer are the initial call and the failure handling in cases where a service call fails due to a lack of privileges. Similarly, using the trust model, the skeleton can hide the selection of a device that is suitable to perform access control. With the exception of the definition of a role specification and the API calls to validate the roles, secure role assignment is completely transparent.

5.5 Applications

In the PECES [PEC10] European research project, secure role assignment is used as a basic abstraction to form a smart space. Within the applications considered by PECES the number of devices contained within a single smart space typically ranges between 3 devices (for a simple in-car smart space) up to 10 devices (for an in-house smart space) which often triples once different smart spaces begin to interact. A PECES smart space is established by dynamically distributing three roles for *member*, *gateway* and *coordinator* devices. The coordinator devices are responsible for providing centralized services such as role-based group communication and service discovery. Gateway devices are responsible for connecting the devices of a smart space with other smart spaces and member devices may provide and use services present in the smart space. Using role assignment, the devices in a smart space will start using applications in a secure manner.

The two applications presented here were implemented in the PECES project

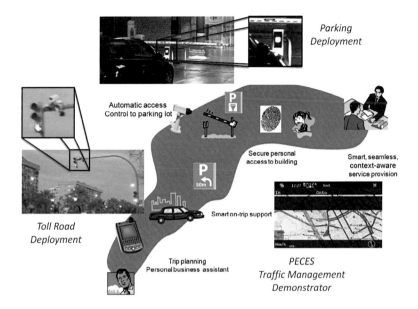

Figure 5.8: PECES Traffic Management Demonstrator

using our approach for secure adaptation with role assignment. The first application is a traffic management application that shows how secure role assignment can be applied to traffic management. It has been implemented by our partner ETRA I+D [ETR]. The second application shows an e-health application scenario. This scenario is particularly relevant for the secure role assignment since personal medical data is usually sensitive data. This application has been implemented by our partner FEA [Fro]. Both scenarios show the applicability of our approach and how it can be used in real-world settings.

5.5.1 Traffic Management

The traffic management application [GM] developed by ETRA I+D and depicted in Figure 5.8 automatically prepares trips on behalf of the user. When a user enters her car, the smart phone automatically extracts the destination from the user's calendar and uses it to configure the navigation system. The navigation system and the user's smart phone use role assignment to limit the access to the user's personal data and services. If applicable, the phone automatically pays road tolls. Additionally, it can be used to reserve parking lots. To do this, the phone determines a suitable parking lot using the secure service registry. This ensures that only trustworthy parking lots are used. When reserving a toll road or a parking lot, the phone transmits the car's license plate which is then used for automated billing. While the car is on the road, the user may subscribe to the latest commercial traffic announcements which are then distributed to all subscribed cars using group communication. Preventing illegitimate access, the data provider uses secure role-based group communication which ensures that only paying customers are able to receive the traffic announcements. To clarify how to involve security rules here, consider the access limitation to the user's personal data. The limitation consists of a role that allows access and checks the following rules: A filter rule *device is allowed access* and a security rule *context issued by a fully trusted device*. This role specification is then injected into the user's smart phone and the access control is managed as pictured in Figure 5.7. Although, the traffic management scenario is fairly complicated and exhibits a number of different entities with varying security goals, secure role assignment provides the basis for realizing all of them.

5.5.2 E-Health

The same holds true for the PECES e-health application [RB] developed by FEA. To clarify this, consider the following excerpt from the e-health application scenario: The e-health application automatically manages the flow of medical data between patients, nurses and doctors as depicted in Figure 5.9. Instead of performing regular visits to remote health care centers, patients are using a mobile device such as a tablet or their mobile phone to keep track of changes to their physical condition. To do this in a semi-automatic manner, the mobile device connects to various sensors in the home. Example sensors may be Bluetooth-enabled scales or thermometers, etc. In addition, the patients make notes about important events such as the amount and type of food that they consumed. Additionally, they may take pictures, e.g., to document skin irritations, etc. The captured data is then regularly synchronized with the medical center where doctors can interpret the data and dispatch nurses. When the nurses receive a request to visit a patient, their mobile device automatically computes the optimal route. Once the nurse enters the patient's home, her device synchronizes with the patient's device to get the latest data. Clearly, given the sensitivity of health related information, it is necessary to ensure that the data synchronization only takes

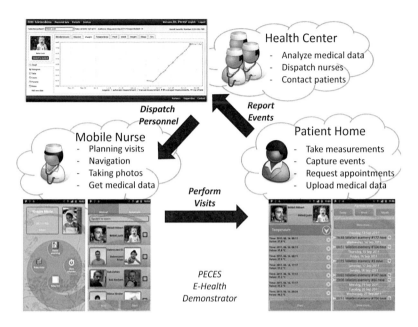

Figure 5.9: PECES E-Health Demonstrator

place with trusted devices over secure connections. To enforce this, the security rules can be defined such that data exchanges are limited to trusted devices as defined by the trust model introduced previously.

5.6 Conclusion

Since distant objects are often less relevant than objects in the proximity, pervasive computing middleware systems typically exploit locality to improve efficiency. Thereby, they introduce artificial boundaries that may become a hindrance. In this chapter, we have shown how generic role assignment can be used as basis for environment adaptations with role assignment. Furthermore, we have presented a prototypical role assignment system. The overhead induced by our implementation indicates that role assignment can be used effectively to exploit locality. At the same time, role assignment allows the expansion of the boundaries in a hierarchically structured way which prevents the introduction of artificial barriers at a low cost.

In many application scenarios, adaptation decisions can have critical security implications. If the adaptation decisions are automated using role assignment, the role assignment must be secured. Thus, we presented secure role assignment as a secure extension to role assignment and we described a prototypical implementation of a system that allows secure adaptation with role assignment. Using this implementation, we showed that the system can provide configurable and secure support to enable the use of role assignment for adaptation decisions even in security critical applications. As indicated by our measurements and further outlined in Chapter 8, given a suitable combination of cryptographic methods, the resulting system is light-weight enough to be applicable to a broad range of devices.

6 Secure Key-Exchange

Before a secure interaction in a smart space or intelligent environment can take place, a key-exchange needs to be performed such that the exchanged key can be used as a basis for encrypted and authenticated communication. In this chapter – *Secure Key-Exchange* – we describe a possible solution to the key-exchange problem. While the previous chapters assumed that devices in the pervasive computing domain are using a conventional certificate hierarchy as a basis for a secure key exchange, this assumption often does not hold true for interactions between users. Instead, users usually verify each other by means of physical recognition. This recognition process can be manifested in the virtual world into a trust link at online collaboration tools. One example is the so-called *friend* relationships on the social network *Facebook*. Our approach PIKE, the *PIggy-backed Key Exchange* and its peer-to-peer variant P2PIKE try to exploit these trust relationships by performing a key-exchange on top of the trusted link in the online collaboration tool. The resulting key can then be used by pervasive computing applications, for peer-to-peer, group and client-server interactions, such as the applications described in this and the previous chapters.

6.1 Preliminaries

Online collaboration tools such as Google+, Facebook or Dropbox have become an important and ubiquitous mediator of many human interactions. In the virtual world, they enable secure remote interaction by supporting restricted sharing of resources such as documents, photos or calendars between users. Users are typically identified with a unique identifier and they authenticate themselves by means of passwords or similar mechanisms.[1] The shared resources can then be tied to different sets of identifiers such as friend lists in Facebook or circles in Google+. To control access to resources, online collaboration tools typically use encrypted communication such as TLS and require authentication upon resource access. Using web-based interfaces, users can access their information from different machines. In addition, many services

---

[1] Examples are two-factor authentication or client-specific certificates.

also provide mobile applications to support access on-the-go and an API for third-party tools to access their resources. Besides providing optimized visualizations, most mobile applications and third-party tools make use of local caching and synchronization to enable disconnected operation.

The success of these collaboration tools indicates that this mediation model can effectively support secure remote interaction. Yet, using them for face-to-face collaboration[2] that takes place in the physical world can be suboptimal. The main reason for this is that such collaboration involves multiple partners that interact with each other *at the same time and place*. In such a setting, the various issues arising from a remote connection – such as higher response times or intermittent connectivity – cannot be hidden by caching and synchronization. A much more efficient way to support online collaboration between co-located partners would be to support their online collaboration by means of short-range wireless communication. However, to provide a similar level of security, this would require encryption and the configuration of corresponding authentication mechanisms. Without a mediating online tool, the co-located interaction partners would have to manually exchange authentication or encryption keys which so far has been too cumbersome to be used in practice.

To avoid this problem, we have designed PIKE, a key-exchange protocol that aims at seamlessly extending the support provided by online collaboration tools to enable wireless collaboration among face-to-face collaborators. The basic idea behind PIKE is to piggyback the exchange of keys on top of the existing service infrastructure of an online collaboration tool in a proactive manner. Thereby, we eliminate the need for manual configuration as well as Internet connectivity when the interaction takes place locally.

A prototype application scenario for PIKE is a business meeting for which invitations are shared over a secure connection using Google Calendar. When detecting the invitations, PIKE automatically exchanges keys over the Internet using the Google infrastructure and stores them locally on each partner's device. When the meeting takes place, the keys can be used to establish secure wireless LAN communication among the participants' devices or to authenticate participants without requiring any Internet connectivity. A second scenario envisions two friends that meet spontaneously in the city. Using their smartphones, they want to interact and transfer data (e.g., pictures) securely. A variant of PIKE, P2PIKE enables them to use automatically exchanged peer-to-peer keys to set up a secure communication.

---

[2]Here, collaboration is not restricted to work context.

The contribution of this chapter is threefold. First, we introduce PIKE and its peer-to-peer variant P2PIKE as approaches for enabling non-mediated, secure and configuration-free face-to-face collaboration. Second, we describe the implementation of PIKE and P2PIKE as an extensible Android library that integrates with wireless tethering to enable the fully automatic establishment of a secure wireless LAN. Third, we present several applications indicating that both PIKE and P2PIKE are broadly applicable and (at least) as secure as the underlying online service(s).

6.2 Approach

Our goal with PIKE is to support local collaboration in a configuration-free and secure manner that does not require Internet connectivity during the time the interaction takes place. To achieve this, PIKE exchanges keys piggybacked on an existing service infrastructure before the interaction takes place. This key-exchange is typically triggered by a virtual representation of the upcoming interaction such as a meeting entry in a calendar. Additionally, it can be performed with all known users of an online service that use PIKE (e.g., Facebook friends running the PIKE app). The exchanged keys can then be used by (pervasive) applications to secure a wireless LAN communication, e.g., by means of encryption or message authentication.

6.2.1 System Model and Assumptions

The technical basis for PIKE are mobile *devices*, such as phones, tablets or laptops that share *resources* with each other remotely through a *network*, mediated by a *service*. Regarding these four building blocks we assume:

- *Services:* The service enables secure restricted sharing of resources. This means that the service authenticates its users, models relationships between different users with respect to resource usage and enables the specification and enforcement of access rights. The service performs its access control to resources properly, meaning that (a) it protects the resources from being accessed by illegitimate users and (b) it allows access from legitimate users. Yet, beyond proper service operation, we do not assume that the service is necessarily trustworthy. Examples may be Facebook, Google+ or Dropbox.

- *Network:* A network such as the Internet enables devices to access the service regularly. The network may be insecure and, occasionally, it may be unreliable or unavailable, e.g., due to a network outage, an incomplete coverage or unaffordable roaming fees.

- *Devices:* The user's device is able to access the service regularly through the network. For this, the service uses a mobile application that synchronizes the changes to a shared resource or provides an API that can be used for resource synchronization.

- *Resources:* Some of the resources shared between users can be read and edited not only by the creator but also by the interaction partners. For PIKE, we assume that some of the shared resources are used to plan a face-to-face collaboration and thus provide time information. Examples for such resources are a calendar entry or a message indicating an upcoming meeting. Using P2PIKE, this assumption can be dropped. In Section 6.2.3, we describe the necessary changes to PIKE.

6.2.2 Design Rationale and Goals

Besides achieving the functional goal of exchanging keys, the desire to maximize PIKE's and P2PIKE's applicability for various types of face-to-face collaboration (i.e., peer-to-peer interactions) defines the following design goals.

- *Full Automation:* To minimize the time required by interaction partners to set up secure communication, PIKE should not require manual configuration. Instead, the key-exchange performed by PIKE should be fully automated such that it becomes transparent to them.

- *High Security*: In order to truly protect the interactions between the devices, the key-exchange performed by PIKE must be secure. Given that the collaboration partners are already using an online collaboration service through remote interaction in order to share resources in a secure manner, the use of PIKE to secure wireless collaboration in face-to-face meetings should result in (at least) the same level of security as offered by the online service.

- *Low Latency:* To avoid situations in which keys are not available for partners, the exchange of keys with PIKE must not introduce a high latency. Specifically, PIKE should be able to provide the exchanged keys quickly after a face-to-face collaboration has been planned, i.e., after a corresponding calendar event has been created or an invitation email has been sent. The key should therefore be exchanged within a few seconds.

- *High Scalability:* As the face-to-face collaboration may involve groups of different sizes, PIKE should be able to support typical group sizes. This means that it should not only be able to provide keys for office scale meetings, but it should also support larger events such as parties with tens of participants (P2PIKE) or scientific conferences with a few hundred participants (PIKE).

6.2.3 Key Exchange Protocol

As explained in Section 6.2.1, the mobile application provided by the service contacts the service and synchronizes recent resource changes regularly onto the user's device. If the mobile application is not present, the PIKE or P2PIKE app can use the API provided by the service to do this resource synchronization. We now describe our two approaches for key-exchange protocols, PIKE and its variant P2PIKE. Both protocols piggyback on services such as online collaboration platforms. PIKE exchanges keys for a group of users. The key-exchange is triggered by a resource (e.g., an event) that is stored at the service. P2PIKE exchanges keys on a peer-to-peer basis with single users of a service. Using our current implementation, both require the users to use a service that is supported by the PIKE application (i.e., Google Calendar or Facebook).

PIKE

PIKE is using an online collaboration platform to support resources like group events. PIKE uses resource changes in online collaboration platforms to trigger key-exchanges. Every time a resource changes, PIKE starts to analyze it in order to detect changes in PIKE-enabled resources that trigger a key-exchange. An example for such resource changes is the creation of an event on Facebook that has been shared with a set of friends and is *marked as shared event* (see Figure 6.1 for more details).

Once a relevant change has been detected, the key-exchange takes place. For this, each partner shares a symmetric key with the creator of the resource, who in turn shares her or his symmetric key with each of the partners. This key-exchange is facilitated by sharing capabilities that are already provided by the service. To do this, PIKE performs either a local modification on the triggering resource or, if this is not possible due to a limitation of the mobile application, it uses the API of the service. Once the changes have been made, PIKE waits for the next resource synchronization at which point all partners will receive the key of the resource creator and the resource

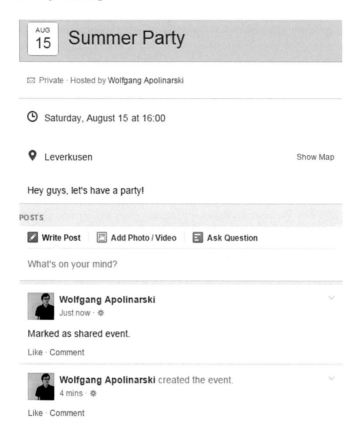

Figure 6.1: PIKE Resource and Trigger in Facebook

creator will receive all keys from all other partners. Once this key-exchange has taken place, these symmetric keys can be used to enable direct secure communication among the devices of the partners.

Figure 6.2 depicts the resulting logical protocol flow which is executed remotely by all partners before the face-to-face collaboration takes place. Conceptually, PIKE involves three entities, namely the device of the partner creating the resource (the initiator), the devices of the remaining partners (the participants) and the online collaboration service. To establish keys, these three entities interact with each other using five steps.

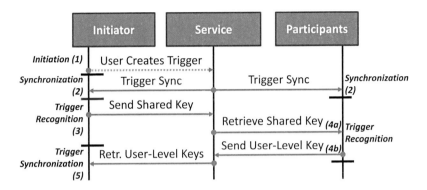

Figure 6.2: PIKE Logical Protocol Flow

1. *Initiation:* The initiator creates the resource that triggers the key-exchange (e.g., an event invitation) using the service's UI and marks it as a PIKE-enabled resource. The mark can be an arbitrary sentence like *Marked as shared event.* (see Figure 6.1 for an example) or any other (possibly hidden) mark that is recognized by the PIKE software. Thereafter, the initiator specifies the set of users (participants) that should be able to access the resource and sets the appropriate access restrictions. The resource is then added to the service which makes it available to the specified users.

2. *Synchronization:* After the resource has been added and shared by the service, the devices of all partners will eventually retrieve the change as part of their normal synchronization process. At that point, the device of the initiator as well as the devices of the participants can access the triggering resource.

3. *Trigger Recognition – Initiator:* The initiator's device recognizes the trigger resource retrieved from the service. The local PIKE process creates a secure key and shares it with all participants simply by attaching it to the resource which will be synchronized with the service again. This key can later be used to protect the communication between the devices of the partners from other entities that are not participating in the interaction (e.g., for secure group communication).

4. *Trigger Recognition – Participants:* After the initiator has attached its key, it will eventually be propagated to the participants. At this point, their corresponding local PIKE processes retrieve the key and store it

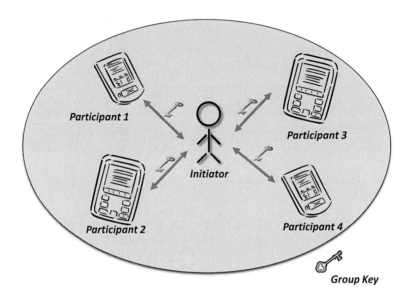

Figure 6.3: PIKE Result

for later use (Step 4a). In order to enable user-level authentication, the PIKE processes on the participants' devices in turn each create a new key and share it with the initiator (Step 4b). Depending on the service, this can be either done by attaching it to the triggering resource or by creating a new resource that is only shared with the initiator.

5. *Trigger Synchronization:* Every time a participant shares a new key (by means of attaching it or by creating a new resource for it), the initiator will eventually receive it on his device. At this point, the PIKE process on the initiator's device learns that this participant wants to join the event, takes the key and stores it for later use (e.g., identification of or secure communication with the participant).

After the completion of these steps all interaction partners possess the key generated by the initiator and the initiator shares a key with each of the participants (see Figure 6.3). Once the face-to-face collaboration takes place, these keys can be used to enable group communication as well as private communication and user-level authentication between the initiator and the participants. The authentication information can then be used to bootstrap

Christoph Baldwyn

Hi! I'm using the P2PIKE app and my public key is:
303E301006072A8648CE3D02010605
2B81040009032A000484DC982EE99D
1D3273EEB6F5244E4976BD831A6C71
B2960A5450B7EB0670DA1FCAC94FCFE67FDE5F

Like · Comment · Share · Promote · 47 minutes ago via PrivacyDH ·

Lara Madelia Hey, my public key is:
303E301006072A8648CE3D020106052B81040009032A0004B39C9A436
1E01D73D2D2C6ECB74A49D34A4B3810364A11A1820287EE430598
15377B04C714A9E8B5

a few seconds ago · Like

Figure 6.4: P2PIKE Resource in Facebook

further keys (e.g., using Kerberos), though the applications described in this chapter do not require this.

To speed up the sequential protocol flow described previously, it is possible to execute Steps 3 and 4b in parallel. For this, the participants share their keys with the initiator immediately after detecting the triggering resource (without waiting for the initiator to share a key). As part of Step 5, they then check for updates on the trigger resource in order to detect the initiator's key as soon as it has been shared. As we describe later on, this simple parallelization can provide a significant speed up.

PIKE distributes a symmetric key for each event resource (i.e., a shared group key) which allows us to support resource constrained devices using symmetric cryptography. Although theoretically possible, in our implementation, we do not support asymmetric key-exchanges (like a group key Diffie–Hellman) here. Asymmetric cryptography could be implemented in PIKE, but would result in a higher processing time. For a similar reason, the individual user-level keys are distributed as symmetric keys (i.e., posted by the participants).

P2PIKE

In general, PIKE uses a triggering resource to support full automation. This automation allows choosing the necessary keys automatically at the time the face-to-face collaboration takes place. In order to drop the assumption of needing a triggering resource, we created P2PIKE, a peer-to-peer version of PIKE which allows exchanging keys with each user individually, i.e., the

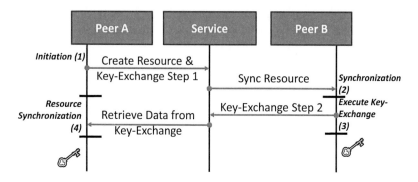

Figure 6.5: P2PIKE Logical Protocol Flow

initiator of an exchange would possess individual keys, one for each user. The exchanged keys can then be used for spontaneous face-to-face collaboration. It depends on the used discovery mechanism (e.g., visual identification of users or the transferring of data between users that includes a user's id) how far automation is supported in P2PIKE.

In contrast to PIKE, P2PIKE is focused on single users (i.e., peers) instead of a group of users. It makes it possible to exchange keys which can then be used for peer-to-peer communication at face-to-face meetings. The usage of the keys is not restricted at all and could be used for the secure exchange of any kind of data. Instead of using a resource to trigger the key-exchange, users can either manually trigger the key-exchange by choosing from a list of P2PIKE users on the online collaboration platform of their choice. Alternatively, they automatically start to exchange keys with all users of P2PIKE that they are related to (e.g., *friends* in Facebook) when they start to use P2PIKE. If P2PIKE detects a key-exchange request from such a friend, it automatically answers the request without user interaction.

As depicted in Figure 6.5, the goal of P2PIKE is the automatic computation of a shared secret key for two peers. Additionally, the service should not be able to passively overhear this key. Therefore, we support asymmetric algorithms like Diffie–Hellman (DH) or ECDH which require two messages that can be executed in the following four steps.

First, an asymmetric key pair (e.g., a DH key pair) is created. Then, similar to the procedure performed by PIKE, P2PIKE will use the mobile application or the API of the service. P2PIKE will – depending on the used online service – attach or create a new resource (e.g., Figure 6.4), adding the public

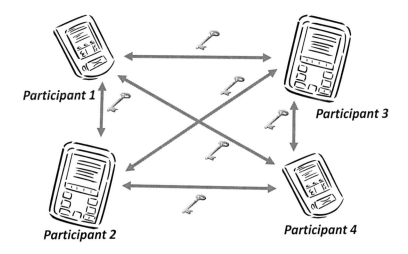

Figure 6.6: P2PIKE Result

key of the created key pair *(Step 1)*. At the next resource synchronization, the peer will pick up the resource *(Step 2)*, create his own key pair and then attach his public key to it *(Step 3)*. In the next synchronization interval, the device that triggered the key-exchange will recognize the attachment from the peer and complete the key-exchange *(Step 4)*.

At this time, both peers can now compute the shared secret key by extracting the other peer's public key from the resource. The key pairs that were created during the key-exchange are not used anymore and deleted after the shared secret key is computed. This key can be used for secure communication similarly to the shared group key that was exchanged using PIKE. In difference to the shared group key, which identifies a communication group, the shared secret key identifies a connection between two peers. If P2PIKE is performed for a group of participants, it results (as can be seen in Figure 6.6) in a peer-to-peer distribution of keys, instead of the centralized (more suited for smart environments like *smart spaces*) approach of PIKE.

At the time a face-to-face collaboration between the two peers takes place, both can use the exchanged symmetric key to establish a secure communication channel using symmetric encryption which is suitable for resource constrained devices. Also note that – in contrast to PIKE – the key itself is never transmitted to the service, but only the two public keys of the used asymmetric key-exchange algorithm.

6.3 Implementation

To validate the concepts of PIKE and P2PIKE, we have implemented both approaches on top of the Android operating system. The implementation consists of activities (i.e., user interfaces) and services (i.e., background tasks) that not only perform the key-exchange but also facilitate secure communication and user-level authentication. As depicted in Figure 6.7, our implementation of PIKE is modular and can support arbitrary services that exhibit the characteristics described in Section 6.2.1 by means of a simple plug-in model. To demonstrate this, we have developed two plug-ins for popular services. The first one taps into the Google infrastructure and uses shared calendar entries as trigger. The second plug-in taps into Facebook and uses Facebook events as triggers. Both plug-ins presented here use the API of their respective services. They are independent of any *app* provided by the service provider (like the Facebook app).

6.3.1 Core Library

The mechanisms of PIKE used commonly across different services are implemented as an Android library (apklib). This core library is responsible for managing the interaction with different plug-ins and it provides functionality to create keys. The latter is used for both the exchanged key for the group (on the initiator's device) as well as the user-level keys. Keys are created using a secure pseudo random number generator that creates 128 bit keys (to support common ciphers such as AES). To further simplify application development, the signaling of a face-to-face collaboration is also implemented as part of the core library. For this, the library manages the meta data such as the list of participants, prospective start and end time, keys, etc. The meta data is represented as a parcelable object which can be passed to the scheduler provided by Android (i.e., the AlarmManager), which fires a notification (a so-called Intent) when the start time has passed – even if the device has gone to sleep. With this meta data, the Android scheduler can automatically trigger further applications.

In addition, the core library also enables applications to set up secure wireless communication among all devices of the interaction partners and it provides the capability for user-level authentication. For providing user-level authentication, it uses a key derivation function and a challenge–response mechanism using a Keyed-Hash Message Authentication Code (HMAC) [KBC97]. For providing secure wireless communication, the core library is capable of establishing a wireless LAN using the tethering capabilities of the Android

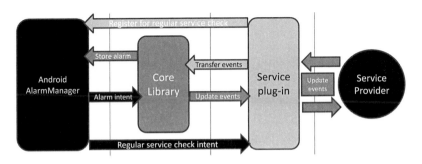

Figure 6.7: PIKE Architecture for Android

operating system.[3] If an application requests secure wireless communication, the group key exchanged via PIKE is used to set up a WPA2 protected network. To do this, all devices present at the face-to-face collaboration derive an SSID as well as a passphrase from the group key. The initiator's device then uses this key to automatically configure and start the tethering mode. The devices of the participants automatically add the configuration to the list of preferred networks, such that the device will automatically join if the network is in the vicinity. While the interaction takes place, the devices can use this network to interact securely. After its completion, the devices automatically remove the network configuration and the tethering mode is deactivated.

Using this functionality, it is easy to build further pervasive applications. However, in order to be useful, the core must be integrated with an online service. To do this, the core relies on plug-ins which realize the recognition of triggers and the attachment of keys.

6.3.2 Google Calendar Plug-in

Google Calendar is one of the most used business services for the management of shared calendars. At work, the calendars can be used to be informed about the absence and availability of co-workers. Meetings can then be planned efficiently and co-workers can be invited to join via the service. Additionally, Google Calendar is pre-installed on most Android phones making it a perfect candidate for PIKE.

---

[3]The tethering capabilities are not part of the API for all Android devices. Yet, the required functions are available on many devices running Gingerbread or higher and they can be invoked via Java reflection.

Figure 6.8: User-level Keys, Posted in an Event in Google Calendar

To access Google Calendar, we use its API to regularly synchronize events between devices and the service. Intuitively, we use shared meetings – appointments with multiple guests – as a trigger for the key-exchange. In order to distribute the key generated by the creator of the appointment (i.e., our initiator), we use a hidden, non-visible field, a so-called *shared extended property*. This field is automatically synchronized with all guests (i.e., our participants) and, if the event is set to private, only guests can see this property. To distribute the user-level keys, we use the comment field of the appointment as shown in Figure 6.8. Again, if the appointment is private and guests do not have the permission to see the guest list, this field cannot be seen by others except by the creator. So using this approach, the initiator can retrieve all user-level keys and the participants can retrieve the coordinator's key by reading the associated fields of the appointment.

6.3.3 Facebook Event Plug-in

Our second plug-in uses Facebook. This online social network service is used mostly for private communication. This usually includes the planning of events or trips with multiple persons. Facebook also provides clients for many different mobile operating systems (e.g., iOS, Android, Windows Phone), so users can stay connected as long as they have network access.

For this implementation, we are using the Facebook Graph API to access and modify data from the social network. As trigger for PIKE we use Facebook events. The participants of events in Facebook can be constrained by the event's initiator. Each event has a private place for discussions only

Wolfgang Apolinarski

Shared event: CAFCD545D3C2A8BD78AA37EAF35DEE
3AA06CFD2E220667AC15121586C1DB52A5

Like · Comment · Unfollow Post · 3 hours ago via CalendarTool

Figure 6.9: Shared Key, at the Event's Wall in Facebook

Stephan Wagner
about an hour ago via CalendarTool ☀

Hi! I'm joining event 194509197395062 with the secret key:
02BB06584A7DF80D864DCB32C7ABD998

Like · Comment

Figure 6.10: User-level Key, at a Participant's Wall in Facebook

viewable by the event's guests, the so-called *wall*. As can be seen by the post pictured in Figure 6.9, this wall is used to post the initiators key that is then automatically picked up by the participants' devices. Since participants cannot change the visibility of posts on the event's wall, the participant keys are posted to the participants' profiles. Each profile has a place for discussion (also called *wall*). On this wall, posts can be created with a privacy setting that constrains the access to the event's initiator (see Figure 6.10). The initiator can then retrieve the participants' keys by going through their walls. For similar reasons, P2PIKE uses a post on a profile's wall as resource. The post can only be seen by the two peers and is deleted automatically by P2PIKE, after the successful execution of the key-exchange.

6.4 Applications

To validate the approach, we have developed a number of applications that apply PIKE or P2PIKE. In the following, we present three of them. The first one performs cooperative context recognition using the devices of the participants of a small to medium-sized meeting. To do this, it requires a low latency, reliable and private network. The second application provides registration services for large-scale events. For this, the application requires secure user-level authentication, but it cannot rely on Internet connectivity. The third one shows how P2PIKE can be used to establish private communication channels that can be used for energy-efficient resource sharing. This application requires a low-latency reliable private network in an environment where no public network (like UMTS or LTE) is available. Both applications are canonical examples that show PIKE's and P2PIKE's capabilities in different conditions.

6.4.1 Privacy-preserving Speaker Recognition

As an example for using PIKE during typical personal interactions at work, we developed a cooperative context recognition application using the context recognition system for mobile devices [IHW+12] developed by Iqbal et al. The goal of this application is to continuously identify the speaker during a meeting, for example to annotate meeting minutes automatically. While this can also be done on a single device by means of voice profiles [LBP+11], cooperative recognition is significantly simpler. Under the assumption that all participants of the meeting are carrying a mobile device, we can determine the speaker by analyzing the different audio streams recorded by the participant's devices. For this, a mobile application running on each device continuously captures sound samples and computes the relevant features like the RMS power value. The features are then transmitted to the initiator's device which uses them to determine the (most likely) speaker for the interval. Once the speaker has been determined, the initiator's device broadcasts the result to the participants which can then use them for annotation and live visualization.

Clearly, for an application like the one described above, the samples and results that are exchanged between the participants of the meeting may contain private information, i.e., the recording of the meeting should not be overheard by eavesdroppers. By automatically exchanging keys via a calendar entry and using them to set up a private wireless LAN during the meeting, we can effectively limit the distribution of samples and results to the actual participants. Similarly, by using local communication as opposed to indirect Internet-based communication, we can rely on the fact that the network will be reliable and fast. This can drastically simplify the application since we do not have to consider issues such as time-synchronization between the devices or retransmissions of high-volume data. Instead, we can simply assume that data will be received quickly and data loss will be infrequent and thus, insignificant.

6.4.2 Configuration-free Conference Registration

As an example for using PIKE in a large-scale event such as a scientific conference, we developed a registration application. At a registration desk for a scientific conference, users register themselves by giving their names, which are then looked up in a list. Using PIKE this time-consuming, error-prone and insecure process can be automated and secured appropriately. To do this, all participants are invited to a Facebook event of the organizers as part of the participant's payment process. When PIKE detects the event, the creator of the event (i.e., the organizer) will provide a key to all participants and the participants will share their user-level keys with the organizer.

At the start of the conference, each participant uses her mobile device to identify herself at the registration desk. To detect the presence of the registration desk, the mobile devices can use the automatic WiFi configuration described previously. On top of that, in order to identify themselves in a secure manner, they send a verifiable message containing their name to the device of the organizer. To create this verifiable message, they compute an HMAC over the message using their individual user-level key which was distributed by PIKE. The organizer can then validate the key and mark the participant as registered.

To perform this process, neither the participants nor the organizers need to perform any manual configuration at the conference site. PIKE detects the shared event days before the start of the conference and exchanges keys. The keys are then used to provide user-level authentication at the conference's start in a fully automated process without needing Internet connection.

6.4.3 Energy-efficient Resource Sharing

As an example for using P2PIKE, we have developed an energy-efficient resource sharing application that aims at supporting the collaborative collection of GPS traces during a hiking trip. Imagine several friends who want to go hiking in the mountains. During their trip, they will not be able to get a reliable Internet connection. Yet, while they are hiking, they want to be able to display their current location in an offline map to support outdoor navigation. Once they have completed their trip, they want to be able to analyze their walking and climbing speeds. To do this, they would like to continuously capture their current GPS coordinates but due to their devices' energy constraints each of the friends can only capture a part of the trip.

Figure 6.11: Energy-efficient Resource Sharing Application (Left: Participant Receiving GPS Readings in Google Maps, Right: Initiator Sending GPS Readings)

Our application mitigates this problem by distributing the energy load generated by the GPS receiver among the friends participating in the hiking tour. To do this, the devices of the hiking friends perform GPS data collection in a round-robin fashion and share the results through WiFi with all other devices. To support the traceability of the GPS data, the data must be authentic. Using P2PIKE, the friends can spontaneously meet for a hiking tour without the need for a triggering resource since they performed the piggybacked key-exchange in advance and can now use the shared keys to establish secure peer-to-peer communication. To do this, the friends can join an insecure WiFi network (e.g., a WiFi hotspot created by one of them) and use the shared keys to authenticate each other. After successful authentication, one of the friends starts sharing his GPS coordinates. He does that by creating a secure network link to each of the friends (using the keys shared with them), transmitting the GPS coordinates over this link. The whole process does not need an active Internet connection, since P2PIKE performed the key-exchange several days before, without needing a physical meeting of the friends or devices.

After joining the network, each friend retrieves the GPS coordinates from the sharer's device and, as can be seen in Figure 6.11, the client application shows the current position (using Android's *mock locations* feature). Our measurements[4] show the following (σ depicts the standard deviation): two devices running only the GPS receiver need each 891 mW ($\sigma = 215$mW; i.e., 1782 mW in total for two devices). Using P2PIKE, it is possible to combine a device receiving the GPS coordinates over WiFi (660 mW, $\sigma = 74$mW) and a second device using the GPS receiver and sending the coordinates over WiFi (935 mW, $\sigma = 148$mW) with a lower total consumption of 1595 mW ($\sigma = 222$mW).

6.5 Conclusion

Exchanging a key for the use in pervasive computing environments can be cumbersome for human users. Online collaboration tools may help the users, because online services have become an important and ubiquitous mediator of many human interactions. In the virtual world, they enable secure interactions by mediating the access to shared resources. PIKE extends the support provided by online services to enable non-mediated secure face-to-face collaboration in pervasive computing scenarios. PIKE is configuration-free and broadly applicable to different scenarios ranging from typical small-scale meetings up to large-scale conferences and events. PIKE and its variant P2PIKE are (at least) as secure as the service used to enable resource sharing.

---

[4]Created using a Galaxy Nexus smartphone running Android 4.2.2, 600 aggregated measurements (1 every 100ms) per point.

7 Automating Policy Generation

Many pervasive computing applications share context between users or devices. To preserve the privacy of users, the applications usually allow the user to define a privacy policy that answers the question *which context should be shared with whom*. This chapter describes a framework that can be used to *automate the generation of a privacy policy* by deriving it from privacy settings that were already defined by users, for example in online collaboration tools such as Facebook or Google Calendar. Often, these settings can be retrieved and then used for the automated policy derivation. In contrast to our previous work that exploited the relationships in online collaboration tools, this work utilizes sharing settings that were already defined by a user to derive an individual privacy policy automatically. The framework that we created simplifies and automates the often complicated privacy policy generation that usually must be performed manually by a user. The generated privacy policy can then be shared among pervasive applications, for example by using the GAMBAS SDK [AIP14] during application development.

7.1 Preliminaries

Nowadays, more and more pervasive computing, crowd-sourcing or participatory sensing applications share context among their users [MLF$^+$08,SHC$^+$12, PBD$^+$14]. Also, commercially available applications (e.g., Windows Media Player) may share context among their users, for example the song the user is currently listening to (e.g., using the Skype or Facebook status message). In the past, the research focus usually lay on the *efficient recognition* of context information. Therefore, privacy concerns were often underestimated, with the major exception of location privacy [WDR12, RB14]. Besides location privacy, also the sharing of other types of context information, especially the disclosure of personal context can have undesirable privacy implications. While a common solution to this problem is the manual creation of a privacy policy, this has several drawbacks. The created privacy policy will be application specific, i.e., not shared between different pervasive computing applications. As a result, the user needs to define a privacy policy for each application. This is cumbersome and can result in an incomplete or inconsistent privacy policy since the user must manually maintain all privacy policies for different context-sharing applications.

Additionally, the user defines several privacy policies when using online collaboration tools such as Facebook or Google Calendar while sharing content with other users. To share content with others, the user usually defines with whom this content should be shared manually, either by adding individual users, predefined user lists or by individually inviting users to events. So, on the one hand, the user already defines an implicit privacy policy for her content. On the other hand, the shared content contains information about the context of a user, for example the current context (e.g., Facebook status messages) or even a future context (e.g., events in Google Calendar). If the type of context is now recognized, it is possible to combine sharing settings and context types to derive a privacy policy that can be applied to context-sharing pervasive computing applications.

Here, we discuss how a privacy policy can be derived automatically by analyzing the user's past sharing behavior when using online collaboration tools like Facebook or Google Calendar. Our approach retrieves shared content and associated sharing settings, detects context types and automatically derives a privacy policy that reflects the user's past sharing behavior. Context-sharing applications can then use this privacy policy directly or offer it to the user as a basis for further customization. In addition, they can frequently update the policy in order to avoid conflicts and minimize inconsistencies. To validate our approach, we have implemented it as an extensible software library for the Android platform and we have developed plug-ins for two popular collaboration tools; Google Calendar and Facebook. To demonstrate and evaluate the library, we discuss its use in a location sharing application.

7.2 Approach

Our goal is to derive a privacy policy from the privacy settings defined in an online collaboration tool like Facebook or Google Calendar. This allows users to *re-use* their previously specified privacy settings for the use with context-sharing applications. Often, users already define their individual privacy needs in online collaboration tools, for example by adding sharing settings to a (shared) resource (e.g., a status message, photo, event). This is usually accomplished by manually choosing the users with whom a resource should be shared. Additionally, groups of other users may be predefined or can be defined manually by the user to ease this process, e.g., allowing to choose a predefined group named *family* instead of selecting each individual family member. In the end, this sharing setting creates an implicit privacy policy for different kinds of resources that can be translated to context sharing settings for applications. Our goal is now to use the resource and the associated sharing setting to derive a general, context-dependent privacy policy for the use with pervasive computing, context-sharing applications such as the applications presented in this thesis here and in the previous chapters.

7.2.1 System Model

For the derivation of privacy policies from online collaboration tools, we require the technical basis described here. Users are sharing *resources* by specifying *sharing settings* in online collaboration tools. Effectively, it is possible to derive *context types* from a resource whose context type could be used by context-sharing applications. The resources are shared with other users using a *network*. Regarding each individual building block, this is the system model, i.e., the list of requirements for online collaboration tools such that we can derive a privacy policy from them:

- Resource: Resources can be shared between users. A resource can be a status message, a photo or similar content shared using an online collaboration tool. Often, a resource describes parts of the current situation of a user.

- Sharing setting: Each resource contains sharing settings that constrain the access to a set of users (e.g., *friends* in Facebook). This setting can be specified by the user. It can be configured individually for each resource.

- Context Type: Since resources in online collaboration tools often describe details of the current situation of a user, they may be used to derive their context types. An example would be a status message resource where the user reveals her current position. Although the type of the resource (e.g., image or text) might influence the context type, there is no direct connection. The type of the context need not necessarily be known by the online collaboration tool, but it should be possible to detect it. Examples of known context type include the *where* field of events in Google Calendar. Examples of unknown context types are status messages in Facebook.

- Network: The resource and the associated sharing settings must be accessible remotely over a network such as the Internet. For this purpose, online collaboration tools usually exhibit an API which can be used by third party tools.

This system model defines requirements that are easily met by many online collaboration tools. A possible example is Facebook with resources such as status messages or events that each define a sharing setting. Since their content can be retrieved, it might be possible to detect their context type. All this data can be reached over the Internet by using the Facebook Graph API. A very similar case is the Google Calendar with events as resources and guests and/or allowed viewers as sharing setting. The context type of a field in an event may be predefined (such as the *where* field), but other fields like the description might have a detectable context type.

7.2.2 Design Rationale and Goals

The overall goal is the derivation of a user-specific privacy policy by analyzing shared resources in online collaboration tools. Therefore, we design a framework for the policy derivation which should be widely applicable. To achieve this, we define the following design goals.

- Generic: Pervasive computing applications use many different kinds of context information. As a result, the framework should be generic with regard to context types. It should support any type and format of context. Additionally, different context scopes (e.g., for location: country, city, street) should be supported.

- Extensible: Besides widely-used social networks like Facebook or online business tools like Google Calendar, there exist many other online collaboration tools. The framework should be extensible such that it is possible to extend the existing framework to support these other tools.

- Automation: In online collaboration tools, users already specify their privacy needs manually using sharing settings. The derivation of the privacy policies should therefore run fully automatic and – if possible – not add further distraction to the user. Additionally, it should support the detection of conflicting sharing settings and present them to the user.

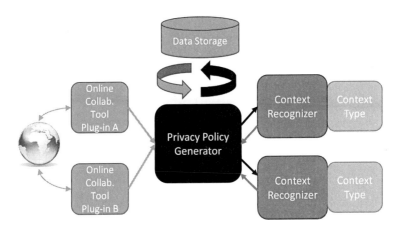

Figure 7.1: Privacy Policy Generation Framework Architecture

- Low Overhead: Manually defining sharing settings in online collaboration tools already needs the user's time and attention. The privacy policy generation should have a low overhead in terms of data transfer and the time that it takes to derive a privacy policy from a retrieved resource.

7.2.3 Privacy Policy Generation Framework

The privacy policy generation framework consists of several components that are combined to derive a privacy policy from online collaboration tools. All components and their interactions are depicted in Figure 7.1. The privacy policy generator has a plug-in interface for online collaboration tools and another interface for context recognizers. Additionally, a data storage is connected to the privacy policy generator to store the derived privacy policy. This allows the framework to support both, different types of online collaboration tools as well as different context types. Using this architecture, the privacy policy generator does not need to know any details about the collaboration tool plug-ins, while the context types (and the associated recognizers) are registered with the generator.

The policy generation can either be executed one-time (e.g., at the first start of a pervasive computing application) or regularly (e.g., to re-check the validity of the current privacy policy). The generation is started when a

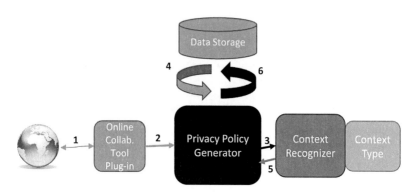

Figure 7.2: Privacy Policy Generation Framework Data Flow

plug-in inputs a resource and its associated sharing settings into the privacy policy generator. The generator then utilizes the registered context types and their recognizers to detect context types from that resource. If the context recognizers detect a context type with a certain probability (definable both by the recognizer and the policy generator), the type and the sharing settings are transformed into a privacy policy and stored in the data storage. If a previous policy for the same context type contradicts the new policy, the new policy is not stored, but can be presented to the user to resolve the conflict. This ensures that only conflict free privacy policies are stored in the data storage. In detail, the privacy policy generation data flow looks as follows (see also Figure 7.2).

1. Resource Retrieval: A plug-in uses the API of an online collaboration tool to retrieve resources and associated sharing settings.

2. Resource Preparation: The plug-in prepares the context type detection by adding meta information to the resource (e.g., possible context types, redundant users (for example users that are added in a group and individually) are removed from the sharing settings). The prepared resource and the preprocessed sharing settings are then transferred to the privacy policy generator.

3. Context Detection: The privacy policy generator receives the resource and sends it to all (relevant) context recognizers. Each recognizer detects the context type (e.g., by using data mining techniques) and associates a probability with a (possible) detection. A recognizer is not

constrained to one context type, but may be able to recognize several different types of context.

4. User Matching: In parallel to the context type detection, the privacy policy generator matches the users contained in the sharing settings with the user database of the pervasive computing application. Users that are not in this database are removed from the settings since they are not using the context sharing pervasive application. Some plug-ins might include an import functionality that allows to import users from online collaboration tools to the pervasive computing application, but for the privacy policy generation, we omit them in this step.

5. Privacy Policy Generation: The privacy policy generator gets the result from the context recognizers, uses the context type with the highest probability (if it is above a predefined threshold like 80%) and generates a privacy policy from the context type and the sharing settings.

6. Storing the Policy: The generated privacy policy is now transferred to the data storage. If the policy conflicts with an already stored policy, the storage marks it as "preliminary" and asks the user to perform a conflict resolution for the newly added, conflicting context types. Preliminary policies are not evaluated during normal operation, i.e., the privacy policy that is used by context-sharing pervasive applications is always free of conflicts.

   If there are no conflicts, or the conflicts were resolved, the privacy policy is stored in the data storage and will be queried when applications want to share context.

The successful execution of these steps results in the generation of a privacy policy containing the context type(s) published at a particular online collaboration tool and the intersection of the users that (a) use the pervasive computing applications and (b) are mentioned in the sharing setting(s).

These steps can be executed several times for each online collaboration tool to refresh the existing policy. Each execution will then extend the policy for an existing context type or add new context types to the policy. The Steps 3 and 4 can be executed in parallel, reducing the time for the privacy policy generation. Similarly, all steps can be executed in parallel with different plug-ins. Only Step 6 must be synchronized between all parallel instances to keep the privacy policy that is located in the storage conflict free.

7.3 Implementation

Validating the concepts of our approach, we have implemented it as an extensible framework. The core part is developed as a library on the Android operating system. Android was chosen since it is an operating system for mobile devices (such as smartphones) that are used by pervasive computing applications. User interfaces are implemented using so-called activities, computations in the background can be either implemented as services (long-running) or as asynchronous tasks (short running, result usually changes the user interface). The prototypical implementation focuses on the context type *location*, but is designed generic which allows support for other context types. Additionally, the extensible implementation includes two plug-ins for popular online collaboration tools. The first plug-in uses *Google Calendar* and evaluates shared events and sharing settings for the calendar, while the second plug-in analyzes status messages of users in *Facebook*.

Our implementation is an instantiation of the theoretical architecture depicted in Figure 7.1. We will start our description of the implementation with the description on how the context types are integrated into the framework. Then, we will describe the privacy policy generator library and two online collaboration tool plug-ins that were created during the implementation.

7.3.1 Context Types and Recognition

As can be seen in Figure 7.3, a context type that should be used within our framework is always associated with at least one context recognizer. This allows the framework to recognize context types from an arbitrary resource (such as a status message or an image). As a result, context types without recognizer cannot be derived from resources and are therefore not considered for the framework. In general, a context type usually describes a single type like *location* and also allows to define scope levels (such as *country*, *city* or *street* using the *location* context type). This enables different context scopes to be used by pervasive context-sharing applications.

For the privacy policy generation, the context recognizers perform an important task, the recognition of the context type from a (Java) object (the resource) that is passed on by a caller. While we do not present context recognizers here, it is possible to add several recognizers to the framework. Possible examples are the NARF activity recognition framework [HIA+10] or other stand-alone (not server-based) recognizers like CenceMe [MLF+08]

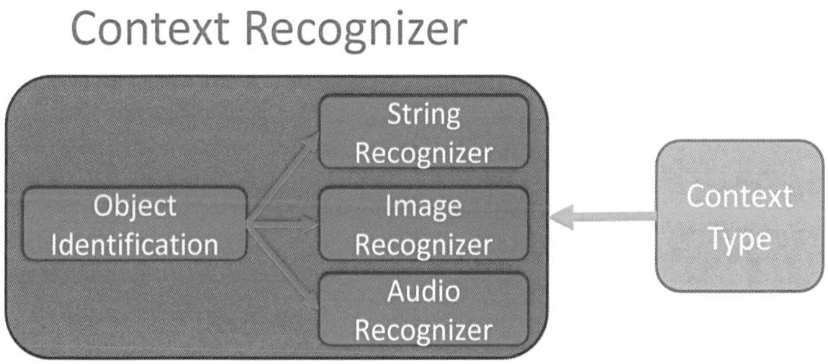

Context Recognizer

Figure 7.3: Context Type with Context Recognizer

that can be executed on Android devices. For privacy reasons, the framework does not include server-/cloud-based context recognizers, because the data would then be transferred to a third party, which contradicts our goal for a better privacy protection. Nevertheless, such recognizers can be included by developers, for example, if the detection is running on a server that is controlled by the user (e.g., a home server). To fulfill the context type recognition task, each recognizer will first identify if the object type is supported and then execute the appropriate recognizer component. The example depicted in Figure 7.3 supports string, image and audio contents. After the appropriate context recognizer has been executed, it will assign a probability to each object type that was passed on. If no appropriate context recognizer exists for this type of object, the probability is 0%. After the recognition finished, the probability will be reported back to the caller.

Eventually, the caller (usually the privacy policy generator) can evaluate all answers received from the context recognizers. Hereby, the caller decides, based on the individual probabilities, which context type should be assigned to the resource, if any.

7.3.2 Privacy Policy Generator Library

The privacy policy generator library is the central element of the privacy policy generation framework. The data flow to and from the generator is depicted in Figure 7.2 and described in Section 7.2.3. To be as flexible as possible, each online collaboration tool plug-in can trigger the privacy policy generator and start the policy generation. This can also be done in parallel,

Permission {
    User 616
    Context type *location*
    Scope 0
}

Figure 7.4: One Permission of the Privacy Policy

only the access to the common data storage component must be synchronized to provide a consistent view on the stored privacy policy.

The privacy policy generator library uses then the transferred sharing settings and reads out individual users. Hereby, the library only extracts users that are allowed to access a shared resource. The reason for this is that our current privacy policy is using a binary grant/deny access scheme on context types. Of course, this model can be extended with a more complex scheme (e.g., involving the time of the day when access to certain context types is granted). After the individual users are read out, a user matching is performed. The user matching process is twofold. At first, only users whose unique account identification for an online collaboration tool (e.g., the Facebook id) that is already known to the framework are considered. In a second step, we perform a more thorough matching, involving the user name and e-mail address. Of course, this can be changed to an even more sophisticated user matching process which involves multiple attributes (e.g., location, birthday, etc.), for example if the names are identical, the unique id is not known and e-mail addresses are not publicly available. This process shows that it is possible to match users even when few attributes are available and it has also proven to be effective [Ali11]. In the end, all matched users are added to a preliminary privacy policy permission object.

In parallel, the privacy policy generator uses the context recognizers to detect context types from the transferred resource. Both information, the detected context type and the users are then combined to one privacy policy element, in our implementation called *permission*. An example can be seen in Figure 7.4. All privacy policy elements together form the privacy policy of the device. An example privacy policy permission that uses the GAMBAS [AIP14] ontology can be seen in Figure 7.5.

At the end, the library stores these permissions in the data storage (usually after user approval, see Figure 7.6), adding them to the privacy policy. The

```
http://eu/gambas/sdk/api/generic/model/Permission/741031972290257236
@rdf:type http://www.gambas-ict.eu/ont/marcus/permission

http://eu/gambas/sdk/api/generic/model/Permission/741031972290257236
@http://www.gambas-ict.eu/ont/marcus/grantsTo
http://eu/gambas/sdk/api/generic/model/Context/7690143230689525234

http://eu/gambas/sdk/api/generic/model/User/6163450586935469790
@http://www.gambas-ict.eu/ont/marcus/hasPermissions
http://eu/gambas/sdk/api/generic/model/Permission/741031972290257236

http://eu/gambas/sdk/api/generic/model/Permission/741031972290257236
@http://www.gambas-ict.eu/ont/marcus/hasLevel "0"
```

Figure 7.5: A Privacy Policy Permission in GAMBAS

Figure 7.6: Screen Showing the Generated Permissions

screen depicted here suggests the user that the context type *location* should be shared with two users. As an additional information, the context detection mechanisms provided a probability of 80%. Conflicting permissions are not added to the privacy policy. Instead, the user is presented a screen to choose which permission should be added to the policy. The privacy policy generated by the library can then be accessed through the data storage by other (pervasive and context-sharing) applications. Using our GAMBAS SDK, the data storage is implicitly accessed by all GAMBAS-enabled pervasive applications, because the query processor is invoking the privacy policy stored in the data storage for every context query.

7.3.3 Google Calendar Plug-in

Google Calendar is a popular tool for sharing calendars between users. It allows to set different levels of calendar sharing. A user may choose to only share her free/busy state, but can also share the calendar completely, including the ability to create appointments in the calendar.

Additionally, the appointments in the calendar contain fields that may exhibit different context information. The *where* field for example indicates that location information is shared, the guest list shows not only with whom this appointment is shared, but could also reveal if this is a private or a work-related appointment.

The Google calendar plug-in uses the Google Calendar API to extract the information and the sharing settings from the appointments and sends it to the privacy policy generator library. If fields with known context types (such as the *where* field) are evaluated, the plug-in defines the context types that will be detected by the library. If other fields (like the *description* field) are evaluated, the library determines the context types (if any). For all detected context types, the library then extracts the set of users the types are shared with and adds the derived permissions to the privacy policy.

7.3.4 Facebook Status Messages Plug-in

Another popular online collaboration tool is Facebook. It is mostly used for private interactions and supports the creation of small statements that describe the current status of a user, so-called *status messages* (see Figure 7.7). Since the messages are usually describing the current situation of a user, they can often be used to obtain context information.

Additionally, the user creating the status message can constrain access to this message by providing sharing settings. Each status message may be shared with a different set of users (called *friends* in Facebook) or lists of users (*friendlists*). The user can also define a default sharing setting that will apply, if she did not specify any custom setting.

The Facebook status messages plug-in uses the Facebook Graph API and retrieves status messages from Facebook. An example JSON response by Facebook can be seen in Figure 7.8. Additionally, the plug-in extracts friends

Wolfgang Apolinarski
Just now

Currently working in Essen. Nice weather today, meet you later in the beer garden!

Like · Comment · Share

Figure 7.7: Status Message on Facebook

```
"privacy": {
        "description": "Marcus Handte, Stephan Wagner",
        "value": "CUSTOM",
        "friends": "SOME_FRIENDS",
        "networks": "",
        "allow": "100001057542495,645219883",
        "deny": ""
},
"message": "Currently working in Essen. Nice weather today,
meet you later in the beer garden!",
"id": "100001039541728_819141028130541",
"created_time": "2014-09-04T14:20:26+0000"
```

Figure 7.8: Graph API Representation of Figure 7.7

that have access to these messages from the sharing settings and also processes friendlists. Each status message and its associated sharing setting can be transferred to the privacy policy generator library to detect possible context types and add them, together with the set of users that is allowed to access these types, as a permission to the privacy policy.

7.4 Application

To validate our approach, we have implemented a location sharing application called *Locator*. The application works similar to the localization components of *LifeMap* [CC11]. It performs the location detection using three different localization methods. It executes a WiFi scan every minute as long as it can detect other devices broadcasting WiFi SSIDs (usually WiFi access points). If the WiFi fingerprint (a vector containing all received SSIDs and their associated RSSI values) changes (i.e., the device is moving), the GSM/UMTS network cell-id together with the WiFi fingerprint is sent every five minutes to the Google location service (over the Android API). The Google location service returns a geo-coded location (i.e., an address including street number) which can be used to extract different scopes of location and allows the application to enrich the user's view of her location history. If no WiFi transceiver is available or no SSID is being received for more than five minutes, the GPS module of the smart phone is used to detect the current location. This is also done every five minutes, as long as no SSIDs are received over WiFi. It is assumed that the user is outdoors, when no SSID can be received and therefore, the GPS module should be able to get a position fix. Each localization method (WiFi, network location and GPS) is executed for a maximum of one minute. If the user's position cannot be detected within one minute, the position is not updated. In summary, the combination of these three different localization methods allows the Locator application to perform an energy-efficient localization of the user. Additionally, Locator supports different scopes for the context type location. E.g., instead of showing the actual GPS coordinates of the position of a user, it is possible to only show the current city. Locator uses the geo-coding abilities of Google's location service to obtain the address and then extracts parts of the address that coincide with the scope the user specified.

In addition to the LifeMap features, Locator allows to share the location between its users, creating an application which works similar to the Google application *Latitude*[1]. The application itself builds on the GAMBAS middleware [AIP14] and uses, amongst other things, the secure communication stack of GAMBAS to perform the communication between users. The middleware also provides Locator with a query processor that is used to query for the location of other users. More details on the GAMBAS middleware and SDK can be found in Section 2.3.2 and in [AIP14].

Since location sharing is sensitive for most users, Locator requires user consent when sharing the current location information. As with similar context-sharing applications, user consent is obtained by a privacy policy that must be edited by the user. The privacy policy generation framework allows to automate this step. When a user now wants to use Locator instead or in addition to manually written status messages to share her current location (see

---

[1] Google Latitude was retired on August 9th, 2013. A similar feature is now offered to users of the social network Google+.

Figure 7.7), she can either manually edit her privacy policy and allow sharing her location with another user, or, use the framework to automatically generate privacy policies (see Figure 7.6) which (usually after user approval) allow the sharing according to the user's previous sharing behavior in online collaboration tools. As soon as the policy is applied, it is possible for users that were included in the policy to retrieve the user's location (see Figure 7.9(a)). Additionally, Locator allows a user to view her own trip history (see Figure 7.9(b)). Since the trip history is only stored on the user's own device, no privacy policy applies in this case. Similar to Google Latitude, Locator does not store the location history of other users, for privacy reasons. It is noteworthy that the Locator app does not share the location with third parties. All location data remains on the user's device and is only shared directly (peer-to-peer) with other users that are granted access according to the user's privacy policy. This privacy feature is unique and does usually not exist in commercial products such as Google Latitude or its successor.

7.5 Conclusion

As described previously, context-sharing applications have become more and more important in the domain of pervasive computing. Often, this has undesirable privacy implications which can be mitigated by using encrypted communication and by defining a privacy policy for each application. As described in this chapter, the user is already defining privacy policies for shared content in online collaboration tools such as Facebook or Google Calendar. These policies can be used for the automated generation of privacy policies for context-sharing applications. The generated policies are then based on the user's previous sharing behavior. This eases the process of defining privacy policies which is often cumbersome for the user. Therefore, we have developed a framework that automatically generates privacy policies out of sharing settings used in online collaboration tools. Frequent re-runs of the tool update the policy, avoid conflicts and minimize inconsistencies. We have shown that our concept is feasible and can, through the support of different online collaboration tools and context types, be extended easily to a wide range of pervasive computing scenarios.

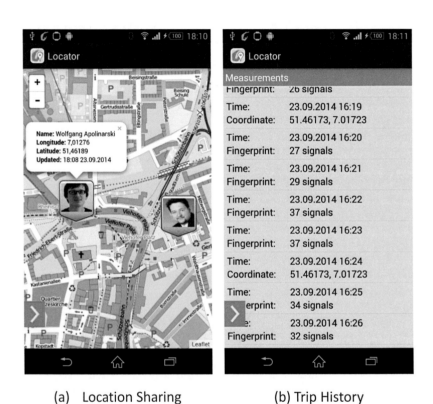

(a)   Location Sharing   (b) Trip History

Figure 7.9: The Locator Location-sharing Application

8 Evaluation

In this chapter, we will revisit the different approaches that we have developed in the Chapters 4 to 7. We are evaluating each approach to the requirements and system model that have been developed in each individual chapter. Additionally, we will show how each approach fits to the requirements that we have created in Chapter 3.

First, we will evaluate the privacy-preserving context management, followed by the secure context distribution framework. Both approaches were thoroughly tested and used during the European project PECES. After this, we evaluate our approach for secure adaptation with role assignment that was also integrated into the middleware created in the PECES project. Then, the secure key-exchange (PIKE) is evaluated. The key-exchange has been integrated in the middleware of the follow-up project of PECES, GAMBAS. Another mechanism that has been integrated into the GAMBAS middleware is our approach for automating the policy generation that is evaluated after PIKE. We close this chapter with a conclusion of the individual evaluations and re-evaluated each approach against the general requirements derived in Chapter 3.

8.1 Privacy-Preserving Context Management

To validate the applicability of the OWL-based model, we used it to model an e-health and a traffic management application in the PECES European research project. Both scenarios shared a number of concepts such as different types of users, sensors, devices and smart spaces. To reduce the modeling effort, we developed a core ontology by combining and extending various established ontologies (FOAF, OWL-S, WGS-84, etc). On top of the core ontology we developed scenario specific extensions. While using the models, we found that even unexperienced application developers where quickly able to define static context characteristics and queries using the open source ontology editor protégé[1] or SPARQL [Worb]. Both scenarios also required the addition of intermediate trust levels which can be seen as an indicator

---

[1] http://protege.stanford.edu

for the need of a privacy-preserving approach. In the traffic management application, sharing the destination was necessary to automatically pay toll roads and parking lots. In the e-health application, the health-related sensor readings had to be shared with nurses and doctors. In both cases the definition of trust levels, certificates and relations was straight forward.

8.1.1 Experiments

We implemented the architecture described in Section 4.1 and used it as a basis for our experiments. In contrast to centralized context management, peer-based context management must be suitable for a broad range of heterogeneous devices. Thus, it is necessary that the concepts can be realized with little resources or that they can be tailored to the devices. To support a broad set of devices, we developed three interoperable context processors.

- **Desktop:** To support desktops that are for instance controlling patients homes, we developed a context storage using Jena[2] and the SPARQL processor for Jena, ARQ which supports processing and the storage of thousands of triples and enables complex reasoning.

- **Mobile:** To provide a storage for less powerful devices such as the smart phones used by a driver or a patient, we created a stripped-down processor by removing unnecessary code from Jena and ARQ. Thereby, we chose a particular database backend which uses a B-Tree for indexing.

- **Embedded:** For embedded devices, such as the actuators in the traffic management scenario or on-body sensors of a patient, we created a minimal context storage without relying on existing libraries. The variant stores triples in-memory and performs an un-indexed query evaluation. It is suitable for 300-500 triples which turned out to be sufficient for our applications.

In order to be interoperable, all implementations share a common lightweight core which encompasses the common interface definition for the context storage service, the objects required to represent RDF triples, SPARQL queries and results as well as the key store and the plug-ins. Together, these components add up to approximately 3500 lines of Java code and an uncompressed binary size of 300KB which is small enough for all platforms supported by the BASE middleware.

---

[2]https://jena.apache.org

```
Q1: select ?device where{ ?device rdf:type device:Coordinator }

Q2: select ?device where{ ?device rdf:type device:Member.
    ?sensor device:linkedTo ?device. ?sensor rdf:type device:SensorDevice.}

Q3: select ?device where{ ?device rdf:type device:Member.
    ?device device:hasAccessory ?accessory.
    ?accessory rdf:type device:Screen.
    ?accessory device:hasResolution ?resolution. ?resolution device:width.
    ?width ?resolution device:height ?height.
    FILTER (width>=240 && height>=320)}

Q4: select ?device  where{ ?device smartspace:hasContext ?locCxt.
    ?locCxt smartspace:relatedLocation ?location.
    ?device service:provides data:printingService.
    ?location spatial:nearby(53.2719172 -9.0525334 100).}

Q5: select ?device where{ ?device smartspace:hasContext ?locCxt.
    ?locCxt smartspace:relatedLocation ?location.
    ?location spatial:within(53.27 -9.05 53.275 -9.055).
    {{?device service:provides data:printingService}
    UNION {?device  service:provides data:otherService} }}
```

Figure 8.1: Classes of Queries

For the performance evaluation, several experiments were performed that measured the storage's response time with regard to different query types and data sets. As basis for this evaluation, we used a PC (AMD Opteron 250, 4GB RAM, Sun JVM 1.6) to test the desktop variant, an HTC Desire (CPU 1GHz, 576MB RAM, Android 2.1) smart phone to test the mobile variant and a SunSPOT (CPU 180 MHz ARM920T, 512KB RAM, 4MB Flash, CLDC 1.1) to test the embedded variant. Based on the two PECES applications (traffic management and e-health), we generated two data sets and we identified five classes of queries with increasing complexity as shown in Figure 8.1.

- **Q1** This query filters the set of known devices for exactly one context (the context *coordinator*).

- **Q2** This query filters the set of known devices which exhibit one context (the context *member*) which also possess a second context that is linked with the first and of a special type (a *sensor*). The list of devices that is retrieved by the first query is therefore further restricted by this query.

- **Q3** This query filters the set of known devices which exhibit one context (*member*) which also possess a second context that is linked with

Dataset	Implementation	Q1	Q2	Q3	Q4	Q5
S1	Embedded	49.06 ms	42.01 ms	3246.30 ms	-	-
S1	Mobile	95.75 ms	60.79 ms	506.67 ms	544.93 ms	35.96 ms
S1	Desktop	1.71 ms	1.41 ms	4.11 ms	9.16 ms	2.84 ms
S2	Mobile	860.92 ms	194.35 ms	3589.34 ms	2156.09 ms	63.60 ms
S2	Desktop	4.24 ms	1.17 ms	12.56 ms	97.09 ms	1.58 ms

Table 8.1: Query Latency

the first (similar to Q2), but further restricts it by applying the *FIL-TER* directive which requires the evaluation (integer calculations) of the given parameters. It searches for devices with a screen size of a certain resolution (at least 240 × 320).

- **Q4** This query filters the set of known devices that exhibit the context type *service* (a *printing service*) near a location specified by GPS coordinates. It contains a spatial query that requires resource-intensive computations.

- **Q5** This query filters the set of known devices for devices in a certain location range (spatial query) that exhibit at least one context type *service* (a *printing service* or an *other service*).

The queries were executed on the basis of two different datasets, *S1* and *S2*. The small set (S1) encompasses 350 triples with 50 devices and 2 smart spaces. The large set (S2) consists of 12000 triples with 2000 devices and 50 smart spaces. As can be seen from the detailed description, the first three queries, Q1, Q2 and Q3 are representative queries for all types of devices. The other two queries only appear on desktop type devices.

Table 8.1 shows the resulting latency. The implementation for embedded devices can easily handle Q1 and Q2. As a result of the non-indexed query processing, the complexity of Q3 increased the latency drastically. Given sufficient memory, it would be possible to decrease the latency significantly by loading all triples into the memory which allows to perform all computations directly in the memory. The implementation for mobile devices can easily handle all queries in the small dataset (S1). In the medium dataset (S2), the latency rises which can be justified by the comparatively large size. The desktop machine can easily handle all queries on both sets. Given these results as well as our experiences with application development in PECES, we are convinced that our peer-based approach to context management can provide a suitable privacy-preserving alternative to centralized approaches.

Requirements	Fulfilled
Peer-to-Peer Infrastructure	
Decentralized	Yes
Highly Scalable	
Generic	Yes
Environment Boundaries	
Configurable	
Flexible	
Composable	
Context Privacy and Security	
Generic	
Reliable Security	
Trust	
Decentralized	Yes
Extensible	
Secure Key-exchange	
Highly Scalable	
User-Level Authentication	
Key Availability	
Individual Privacy Policy	
Generic	
Automated	
Low Overhead	

Table 8.2: Context Management in Comparison to the Requirements

8.1.2 Qualitative Evaluation

When compared with the requirements that we derived in Chapter 3, it can be seen easily (in Table 8.2) that this is a first step to fulfill the peer-to-peer vision of pervasive computing. It does not include any security algorithms related to context security, but already provides the necessary mechanisms for a decentralized peer-to-peer infrastructure, including decentralized trust. By supporting three different types of devices, our query processor is running resource-aware, additionally supports generic ontologies and is therefore generic with regard to the type of context.

8.2 Secure Context Distribution Framework

In the following, we evaluate the secure context distribution framework by revisiting the requirements that we identified in Section 4.2.4 and the general requirements derived in Chapter 3. We first discuss the qualitative characteristics. Thereafter, we provide a set of benchmarks to quantify the resource utilization.

8.2.1 Discussion

Due to the fact that the context update messages issued by the framework explicitly identify the source and the target of the context information by means of fingerprints, there is a strong association between the generator and the storage. By authenticating the storage and the context information during validation, some other storage cannot illegitimately use the context information. As a consequence, the context distribution framework supports the utilization of devices that are not trustworthy per se and thus, it allows decentralized operation.

Our validation framework is generic as it can be used to distribute any type of context since the services do not make assumptions on the data representation. In our current implementation, the services use byte sequences with equality matching. Yet, the integration of more complex type systems and matching operators would be straight forward.

With respect to reliable security, the signatures ensure that the context information cannot be altered and that a storage device must possess the appropriate private key to use the context. While this prevents attacks such as copying or modifying the context information, the presented framework cannot stop a device from sharing its private key which makes devices indistinguishable. For example in the scenario introduced in Section 4.2.3, a visitor that legitimately passed the gatekeeper could share the context information with an intruder that jumps over the fence. However, if the visitor and the intruder are cooperating, the visitor could also simply use his storage device to open the door for the intruder. Thus, it is not possible to prevent such attacks technically by solely using cryptography in general. The second possible attack that is not prevented by the framework is a relay attack in the validation protocol. Instead of responding directly to the request message, an intruder could simply forward it to the legitimate storage that holds the context. Once the legitimate device responds, the intruder then forwards the response to the validator. When the message arrives at the validator, the validation succeeds since the validator actually validates the legitimate device. Yet, for this attack to work, the intruder must mask as the legitimate device (e.g., by copying the fingerprint) and it must be connected to both, the legitimate device and the validator device, simultaneously. From a scenario perspective, this is similar to an intruder that is slipping through the door that has been opened by a legitimate user. Thus, it is possible to complicate such attacks by reducing the communication range. From a protocol perspective, it is possible to initiate the validation on the storage device or to have the user accept an incoming request message manually (such that she gets aware of any relay attack attempts). As a result, the attack would no longer be possible or could be detected at the price of an increased level of manual interaction.

With respect to configurable trust, the framework enables validators to freely model trust on the devices of different administrative domains by means of a configuration of the key store. Due to the use of asymmetric cryptography, it is possible to model unidirectional relationships as well. This is especially useful in the context of business environments where the devices of an employee may trust the sensors of the company but not vice versa. In addition to the not-trusted and trusted categorization performed by our current prototype, it would be straight-forward to integrate a less coarse-grained notion of trust by introducing detailed classification of root certificates in the key store.

8.2.2 Measurements

As can be seen in Table 8.3, on a SunSPOT[3] (CPU 180 MHz 32bit ARM920T core, 512KB RAM/4MB Flash, J2ME CLDC 1.1 Java VM), processing a standard Diffie-Hellman key exchange, which requires two cost-intensive computations, using the Bouncycastle [The] library required more than 2 minutes. By applying elliptic curve cryptography using a highly optimized library provided by Sun we were able to reduce this overhead to under a second. Table 8.3 shows the overhead for the primitives used in our current implementation on a SunSPOT as the mean value of 20000 runs for the HMAC, 200 runs for ECC computations and 100 runs for ECDH and DH. In the end, the performance of the optimized ECDH key exchange implementation results in a mean of less than 1 percent of the mean of DH on SunSPOT devices.

---

[3]http://www.sunspotdev.org

Cryptographic Operation	Mean (95% Conf. Int.)
HMAC-SHA1 (Sign/Verify)	11.34 ms (8.98 ms, 13.69 ms)
ECC Sign (Optimized, SECP160R1)	644.57 ms (473.14 ms, 816.00 ms)
ECC Verify (Optimized, SECP160R1)	796.07 ms (607.12 ms, 985.01 ms)
DH (Bouncycastle, 1024 bits)	61224 ms (61136 ms, 61313 ms)
ECDH (Bouncycastle, SECP160R1)	22927 ms (22715 ms, 23138 ms)
ECDH (Optimized, SECP160R1)	524.33 ms (511.92 ms, 536.75 ms)

Table 8.3: Context Distribution Framework Cryptography Costs

To quantify the resource utilization of the framework, we installed our prototypical implementation on SunSPOT devices (using the RED SDK) and we computed a series of benchmarks shown in Table 8.3. In the following, we describe the performance of the protocol in the worst case, i.e., all measurements are based on SunSPOTs, which are taken as an example of a resource-constrained device. When the task of the validator, storage or generator is operated by a device with higher computing capabilities, such as a smart phone or PC, the measured delays decrease drastically. Demonstrating the suitability of the framework even for small devices such as SunSPOTs, we evaluated the worst case. As a basis for the computed delays, we used the mean values from Table 8.3.

When some piece of context information shall be distributed (as depicted in the distribution protocol in Figure 4.4), a generator must create a single signature (SIG_G) in addition to the transmission of the context information which results in an additional overhead of 644.57 ms (One execution of an *ECC Sign* operation). By using the symmetric mechanism, this overhead can be reduced even further to 11.34 ms (One execution of an *HMAC-SHA-1* operation). If the storage wants to perform the optional validation of the signature (i.e., validate the signature of the generator, SIG_G, on the update as well as the generator's certificate, $CERT_G$), it needs to perform 2 validations which increase the delay by 1592.14 ms (2 executions of *ECC Verify*). This results in a total delay of 2236.71 ms if the generator is using the asymmetric mechanisms and 1603.48 ms, if it is using the symmetric approach (that is bound to one infrastructure and needs a bridge device or collaborating generators and validators as described in Section 4.2.5).

To use a previously distributed piece of context information (depicted in the validation protocol, Figure 4.5), a validator must first generate the signed request (SG_V) and then it needs to perform one validation of the storage

Requirements	Fulfilled
Peer-to-Peer Infrastructure	
Decentralized	Yes
Highly Scalable	Partially
Generic	Yes
Environment Boundaries	
Configurable	
Flexible	
Composable	
Context Privacy and Security	**Yes**
Generic	Yes
Reliable Security	Yes
Trust	
Decentralized	Yes
Extensible	
Secure Key-exchange	
Highly Scalable	
User-Level Authentication	
Key Availability	
Individual Privacy Policy	
Generic	
Automated	
Low Overhead	

Table 8.4: Context Distribution in Comparison to the Requirements

(validate the storage's signature SIG_S) and two validations of the contained update (validate the generator's signature SIG_G and certificate $CERT_G$) which results in a total overhead of 3032.78 ms (1 *ECC Sign* operation, 3 *ECC Verify* operations). In addition to that, the storage must also create a signature for the response (SIG_S) which corresponds to 644.57 ms (1 *ECC Sign* operation). If a storage wants to validate the request, i.e., validate the validator's certificate $CERT_V$ and signature SIG_V, this introduces another 2 validations (2 *ECC Verify* operations) and increases the delay by another 1592.14 ms. The total delay for the validation is therefore 5269.49 ms, if the storage is verifying the validator and 3677.35 ms, if it is not verifying.

As a consequence, the total overhead for context distribution and usage boils down to 7506.20 ms (3 *ECC Sign* operations and 7 *ECC Verify* operations), if the storage performs all validations and 4321.92 ms (3 *ECC Sign* operations and 3 *ECC Verify* operations), if the storage simply accepts all updates and requests. Clearly, this overhead makes it impossible to use the framework for context information that is changing at a high rate. However, if the context exhibits this behavior, it is likely that the context generator and the context consumer are directly connected. Thus, it is easier to ensure the validity of context by securing the connection. In cases, where direct connections are not possible, the additional overhead for context that needs to be secured is not unreasonably high. As a consequence, we argue that this approach is applicable to a broad range of scenarios.

8.2.3 Qualitative Evaluation

When we compare the secure context distribution framework with the requirements derived in Chapter 3 (see Table 8.4), we can see that – in contrast to our previous work – this framework includes security mechanisms with regard to context security. Although it is applicable to a wide range of devices, its scalability is limited due to the use of asymmetric cryptography which is resource-intensive and therefore not well-suited for resource-poor devices. While the use of so-called bridge devices overcomes this issue, the integration of these devices is complicated. The high scalability is therefore only given in some scenarios and marked as *Partially* for partial support. Regarding context security, the framework fulfills high security standards by using elliptic curve cryptography (ECC) and an SHA-1-based HMAC. Additionally, it supports decentralized levels of trust by establishing peer-to-peer trust based on certificates. In summary, the secure context distribution framework can be regarded as a further step to the vision of secure pervasive computing environments.

8.3 Secure Adaptation with Role Assignment

To evaluate our approach for secure adaptation with role assignment, i.e., the secure role assignment system and the associated services, we now discuss the requirements derived in Section 5.2 and then compare them with the general requirements derived in Chapter 3. We relate them to our experiences in the PECES European research project where we developed several security critical prototype applications for various scenarios including traffic management and e-health that were described in detail in Section 5.5. At first, we show that secure role assignment provides us with a *configurable, composable, flexible, secure* and *light-weight* abstraction. Thereafter, we present a number of experiments that support the statement of our approach being light-weight. The evaluation indicates that secure adaptation

```
SELECT ?device
WHERE
{
        ?vehicle <http://www.ict-peces.eu/ont/smartspace.owl
        #participatingDevice> ?device.
        ?vehicle <http://www.ict-peces.eu/ont/smartspace.owl#isOwnedBy>
        <http://www.ict-peces.eu/ont/smartspace.owl#JohnSmith>
}
```

Figure 8.2: Role Specification (SPARQL)

with role assignment is flexible enough to support a broad range of services and applications without introducing high performance overheads.

8.3.1 Configurable

The applications that were described in Section 5.5 show that secure role assignment is applicable to two completely independent scenarios, here traffic management and e-health. Of course, because role assignment is just a basic abstraction for automatic adaptation, these applications require the provisioning of additional services on top, but the easy realization using secure role assignment is a clear indicator for fulfilling the design goals of having a flexible, *configurable* abstraction.

To support an easy configuration, it is possible to reuse pre-defined ontologies. This allows a developer to directly start with the definition of the necessary roles. Additionally, it is also possible to extend an existing ontology as well as creating a new ontology, if desired. Our approach and prototypical implementation does not constrain the layout of the ontology. Instead, a developer may freely create the ontology, RDF triples and SPARQL role definitions that are necessary for the scenario(s) and may specify arbitrary filter and reference rules that can be evaluated automatically at runtime. An example SPARQL role used in the traffic management application is pictured in Figure 8.2. The role selects all devices in *John Smith*'s car that he also owns. Although it is possible for a developer to define roles in the SPARQL language, we also created a role specification editor (Figure 8.3) that eases the configuration process especially when creating complex role specifications for feature-rich smart spaces.

8 *Evaluation*

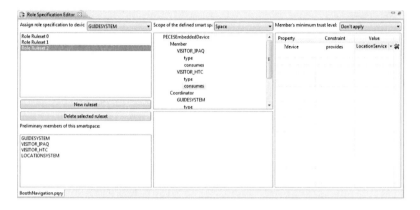

Figure 8.3: Role Specification Editor

8.3.2 Composable

As described previously, our approach for secure adaptation with role assignment is not limited to a single role specification. Instead, multiple specifications may be developed independently and executed simultaneously. The support for reference rules within role specifications enables the hierarchical composition of environments. By supporting the hierarchical composition, role assignment can be used to dynamically extend existing environments in a controlled fashion. In Section 5.5, we presented two applications that use the hierarchical composition, allowing independent smart spaces (like a car smart space and a parking lot smart space) to interact with each other.

8.3.3 Flexible

Environment or smart space configuration with role assignment is not primarily based on the context type location. Instead, it enables developers to define boundaries using properties of the device context. Clearly, in order to use a property in a role specification, it must be available on the relevant devices. However, when looking at the increasing number of sensors that are deployed in current smart devices, it is conceivable that many devices will be able to perceive a large part of their context. As a result, role assignment increases the flexibility of environment configuration when contrasted with the locality-based approaches.

146

8.3.4 Secure

We are providing Internet-level security in our prototypical implementation. In detail, we are using 160-bit ECC certificates for the device authentication and elliptic curve Diffie-Hellman (ECDH) to derive a 256-bit session key (using SHA-256). For the prototypical implementation, we split this session key into two 128-bit keys. The first key will then be used to encrypt the data transfer with AES-CBC while the second key is preserving the integrity with an SHA-1-HMAC. Since both the encryption and the integrity check rely on symmetric cryptography, their execution is fast, even on resource constrained devices like smart phones.

The role assignment process requires a secure connection, when security rules exist. Additionally, roles that are validated by another device than the role-issuing device are either signed asymmetrically or (preferable, since faster) symmetrically (using an HMAC, not a cryptographic signature). The roles can then be validated as described in Section 5.3.6. The approach itself was used in PECES and is independent from the mechanisms that were used in the prototypical implementation which shows its feasibility. The modular structure of our middleware allows an easy replacement of the security implementation to adapt to higher (or lower) security requirements although the current implementation still provides Internet-level security strength and therefore supports the formation of smart spaces through insecure networks like the Internet.

As described in Section 5.3.4, we are supporting different models of trust. The model that we are using in our prototypical implementation builds on the conservative approach of certificate hierarchies. In the two applications discussed in Section 5.5, certificate hierarchies are a flexible and reliable mechanism. To ease the administration of the hierarchies, we also developed a hierarchy editor similar to the role specification editor that was described in Section 8.3.1. Our experiences during the development of the applications showed that this allows also unexperienced developers to create a secure certificate hierarchy for their enterprise environment.

Using our approach, all devices can decide independently, if they trust other devices. Of course, the use of certificates is limited since devices that were taken over by a malicious person might still have access to a valid certificate, if certificate revocation lists (CRL) are not distributed thoroughly. Allowing the validation of certificates of a certain authority only when a recent CRL is available minimizes the attack window, but also requires all devices to have a connection to the certificate authority, from time to time. A similar problem might occur, if a reputation-based trust system is used and a device with a high reputation starts acting maliciously. Nevertheless, also a dynamic, trust and risk-based framework [CGS$^+$03] can be used in our approach, replacing or extending the certificate hierarchy based trust model in our prototype.

8.3.5 Light-weight

As described in Section 5.4, the prototype was implemented in Java. This allows us to test our approach on a broad range of devices. During the development of the prototype, we tested it on several types of devices to make sure that it is applicable to all of them. To provide a thorough analysis, in the following Section 8.3.6, we provide measurements on how our prototype performs on low-end smart phones. We are showing the penalty introduced by the security mechanisms as well as the overall role assignment performance. These experiments show that our approach is light-weight.

8.3.6 Experiments

During the development of the applications in PECES, we have used our system for the secure adaptation with role assignment on a broad variety of devices. This includes both, resource-rich devices such as traditional servers, laptops and tablets as well as resource-constrained systems such as phones, WiFi routers (running OpenWRT) and sensor nodes (i.e., SunSPOTs). Throughout the development and testing, we found that the resulting application performance was not impacted in a dramatical way. Measuring the general feasibility of our role assignment approach, we show first some measurements that use the role assignment methods presented here, but do not include security. After that we present experiments in which we show the overhead of the security in detail.

Generic Role Assignment

For all experiments that do not include security, we use the following hard- and software configuration consistently. We use an off-the-shelf Asus EEE PC T91 (Intel Atom Z520 1.33 GHz CPU, 1 GB RAM) running Windows XP and Sun JRE1.6 to perform assignments and we connect it to a varying number of devices. For this, we use HTC Tattoos (Qualcomm MSM7225 528 MHz CPU, 256MB RAM) running Android 1.6. To connect the devices, we use an IEEE 802.11g wireless network hosted by a Netgear WNR3500L access point which is used exclusively for the experiments.

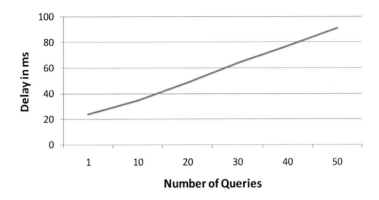

Figure 8.4: Latency with Varying Number of Queries

To validate that the system can be used on resource-poor devices, we measured the binary size of the additional Java code. Using our minimal context service implementation that does not use JENA and ARQ, the services require an additional memory space of 140KB. However, this space can be reduced to 85KB if a system does not have to perform role assignment. Thus, the role assignment system supports a broad range of devices including phones or embedded devices such as Sun SPOTs.

The performance of role assignment depends on the contents of the role specification. The two primary influential factors are thereby the number of queries in filter rules and the number of roles that shall be distributed. In order to measure the impact of these factors, we performed two experiments which vary them systematically. In both experiments, we execute the role specifications 200 times with one HTC Tattoo and we measure the delay experienced for performing a single assignment. The standard deviation is indicated with σ.

Figure 8.4 shows the results of the first experiment for which we create a role specification consisting of one role that contains a varying number of queries for one RDF triple (1-50). Figure 8.4 indicates a linear growth of the average latency for role assignment starting from approximately $24ms$ ($\sigma = 11ms$) when one query is attached up to approximately $91ms$ ($\sigma = 16ms$) when 50 queries are present. Due to the batch processing for query execution, this increase can be explained by the increased effort for serialization, transmission and remote execution.

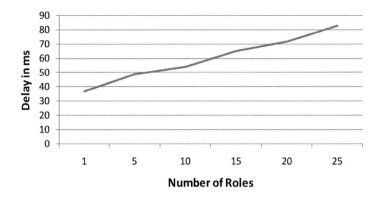

Figure 8.5: Latency with Varying Number of Roles

To evaluate the effects of an increasing number of roles, we use the same setup with one device but we change the role specification to contain a varying number of roles (1-25). Thereby, each role queries one triple. Similar to Figure 8.4, we can observe a linear increase in latency for performing the role assignment as depicted in Figure 8.5. However, the increase is approximately twice as steep with a absolute latency of approximately $83ms$ ($\sigma = 52ms$) when distributing 25 roles. Similar to the experiment that varies queries, we can attribute this to the increased effort for serialization, transmission and execution. The reason for the higher increase results from the fact that each role also contains one query.

We conclude from these two experiments that increasing the number of roles or the number of queries result both in a linear increase of the latency experienced in role assignment. Thereby, the absolute values of less than $100ms$ clearly indicate the suitability for comparatively resource-poor devices. In order to measure the effects of an increasing number of devices, we have performed two additional experiments. In the first one, we measure the overhead for evaluating filter rules. In the second one, we measure the overhead for hierarchical assignment using reference rules. In each experiment, we measure 200 role assignments and compute the average role assignment latency.

Figure 8.6 shows the effects on latency when increasing the number of devices in an assignment that uses filter rules. The role specification in this experiment consists of one role with one filter rule that queries a single con-

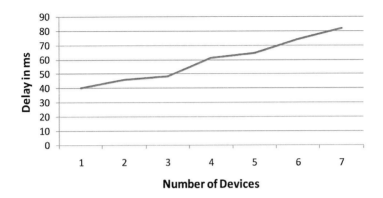

Figure 8.6: Latency for Filter Rules with Varying Number of Devices

text property. As indicated in Figure 8.6, increasing the number of devices also increases the latency. However, when comparing the absolute values it becomes apparent that an increase in the number of devices only causes a comparatively marginal increase in the overall latency. For example, the role assignment with 2 devices is less than twice more expensive than with 1 device. The reason for this can be attributed to the fact that the filter rules contained in the role specification can be executed on the devices in parallel. However, in practice the achievable gain from this parallelism also depends on the amount of data that is transferred. Thus, for an increasing number of devices, the increase in latency would eventually approximate direct proportionality due to network saturation.

As shown in Figure 8.7, such effects are not present when a specification contains only reference rules. In the experiment depicted in this figure, we evaluate the latency for assigning a role to a varying number of devices on the basis of an existing role. The reference rules used in this experiment reference two role specifications that are running in the system. In order to show the actual effort for evaluating the reference rule, we do not measure the delay for device notification. Due to the fact that the computation of the assignment can be done completely locally on the assigning device, the overall time for assignment stays well below $10ms$ for all experiments. This clearly indicates the usefulness of reference rules and it also demonstrates the effectiveness of hierarchical composition, especially when forming a group from existing groups.

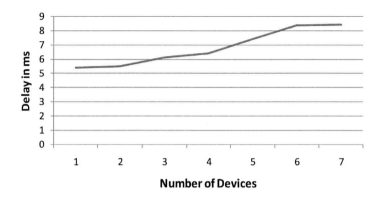

Figure 8.7: Latency for Reference Rules with Varying Number of Devices

In most settings, however, we would expect to see a combination of reference and filter rules which would prevent a purely local evaluation. Yet, in these cases, our implementation restricts the number of devices that must evaluate the filter rules to those that already posses the desired set of roles. Thus, instead of contacting all nearby devices, the device performing the role assignment only has to contact a subset. Given the low effort of reference rules, this approach is often beneficial.

Note that we can simply compute the overall effort for such more realistic settings from the synthetic measurements. Since the delays shown in Figure 8.7 do not contain the delay caused by notifications, we can directly sum up the efforts for hierarchical assignment shown in Figure 8.7 with the effort shown in Figure 8.6. As described previously, within the scenarios considered by PECES the number of devices contained within a single space typically ranges between 3 devices (for a simple in-car smart space) up to 10 devices (for an in-house smart space) which often triples once different smart spaces begin to interact.

In a medium-sized smart space that consists of 6 devices where roles are distributed using one filter rule each, the total overhead introduced by role assignment can be estimated as follows: The total time to set up the environment is computed from the execution of the three queries ($26ms$), the distribution of 8 roles (6 member, 1 gateway and 1 coordinator, $52ms$) and the role assignment latency for 6 devices ($74ms$). This adds up to $152ms$ for each setup. To detect changes, the role assignment is performed at regular

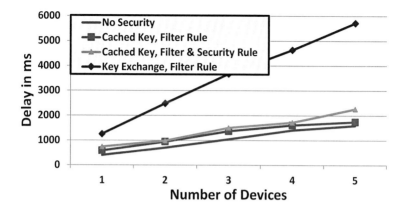

Figure 8.8: Secure Role Assignment Delay

intervals of 30 seconds. Thus, the overhead introduced by role assignment in this case is well below 1 percent.

Secure Role Assignment

For the security experiments, we used a Lenovo T61 laptop (Intel T5670 1.8 GHz Dual-Core CPU, 3 GB RAM) running Windows 7 and the Oracle Java JRE 1.7 to perform all secure role assignments. The laptop is connected to a varying number of HTC Tattoo devices. On each device, an individual 160-bit ECC certificate is pre-deployed. According to Bos et al. [BKK+09], the security provided by 160-bit ECC is at least as high as 1024-bit RSA, a standard that is widely used in the Internet. For the wireless connection, we used again a dedicated IEEE 802.11g network. All measurements show the average delay of 100 repetitions and take not only the execution of the security rule, but also the assignment of the role containing this rule into account. This includes the network transfer overhead and execution of all security protocols (e.g., signature/HMAC verification) on the role issuer's and receiver's side, i.e., shows the total overhead. Again, the standard deviation is indicated with σ.

As a baseline (*No Security*), we measured the total delay of assigning a single role to a varying number of HTC Tattoos. The resulting delay is depicted in Figure 8.8. The time shown is the total time that passes between starting a role specification on the laptop until all devices have received the role. For 5 HTC Tattoo devices, the total time stays well below 1.6 seconds ($\sigma = 175ms$). The second (*Cached Key, Filter Rule*) and third cases (*Cached Key, Filter and Security Rule*), show the overhead for role assignment if the resulting roles shall be transmitted securely to their receivers but the key to establish a secure connection has been cached already. As can be seen from the measurements, the additional encryption (128-Bit AES) adds a small overhead to the overall process. This overhead is increased by the addition of a filter rule, as this requires the additional validation of an (asymmetric) signature on the laptop. With at most 2.3 seconds ($\sigma = 793ms$) for role assignment with 5 devices the total overhead remains low. The last measurement (*Key Exchange, Filter Rule*) is identical to the second case, but in addition, it requires the exchange of a key using ECDH. As depicted in Figure 8.8, the key exchange drastically increases the overhead to 5.8 seconds ($\sigma = 329ms$) for 5 devices due to the high computational effort for ECDH. However, due to the fact that the key store can cache the resulting symmetric key between different interactions, this overhead is only experienced once. With an approximate overhead of less than 1 second per device for the key exchange, we are argue that secure role assignment is *light-weight* and can be applied in many scenarios.

8.3.7 Qualitative Evaluation

Many approaches for security systems in the pervasive computing domain introduce a central server responsible for security. As described before, this contradicts our view of a smart space or pervasive environment which consists of decentralized applications and services. Therefore, a centralized approach for security is not suitable. Although we support re-active secure role assignment with the possibility to externalize secure role assignment to another device in the environment, there is no central security service and the infrastructure is therefore fully decentralized. Similarly, with the use of filter and references rules, the secure role assignment presented here, can create smart spaces using flexible boundary definitions.

When compared to the requirements that were derived in Chapter 3, we conclude that our approach for a secure role assignment system has fulfilled the items *Peer-to-Peer Infrastructure, Environment Boundaries, Context Privacy and Security* and *Trust* as can be seen in the last column of Table 8.5. There, we also show the combined requirements evaluation of our approaches for context management and distribution that were integrated into the secure role assignment. With regard to trust, the architecture of the

Requirements	Context	Fulfilled
Peer-to-Peer Infrastructure		**Yes**
Decentralized	Yes	Yes
Highly Scalable	Partially	Yes
Generic	Yes	Yes
Environment Boundaries		**Yes**
Configurable		Yes
Flexible		Yes
Composable		Yes
Context Privacy and Security	Yes	**Yes**
Generic	Yes	Yes
Reliable Security	Yes	Yes
Trust		**Yes**
Decentralized	Yes	Yes
Extensible		Yes
Secure Key-exchange		
Highly Scalable		Partially
User-Level Authentication		
Key Availability		
Individual Privacy Policy		
Generic		
Automated		
Low Overhead		

Table 8.5: Secure Role Assignment in Comparison to the Requirements

secure role assignment system is flexible and allows to deny devices the access to sensitive information, simply by setting their (root) certificate to *no trust*. The context privacy and security is ensured by binding certificates to devices. Additionally, a cryptographic signature is used, which protects the integrity and authenticity of context. The key-exchange allows to support encrypted communication to secure the transfer of context information, but is only partially scalable and can only be used in pervasive computing scenarios which are based on machine-to-machine communication. In summary, our approach for secure adaptation with role assignment is only missing an approach that fulfills our requirements with regard to secure key-exchanges and an individual privacy policy that controls the (possible) sharing of context information.

8.4 Secure Key-Exchange

In the following, we evaluate our secure key-exchange mechanism PIKE and its variant P2PIKE along the four design goals that we introduced in Section 6.2.2 and against the requirements that were derived in Chapter 3. The design goals are *full automation, high security, low latency* and *high scalability* and extend the derived requirements. Next, we discuss each of them.

8.4.1 Full Automation

The key-exchange with PIKE does not require manual interaction. Nevertheless, to establish a key using PIKE, it is necessary for all participants to use a third-party service (e.g., Facebook). Also, the initiator needs to create the shared trigger condition (i.e., an event) using this service and adds the guests or group of guests manually using for example the service's web interface. However, managing events and inviting guests are necessary steps that always need to be performed by an event creator, even when not using PIKE. Regarding P2PIKE, no manual interaction is necessary when keys should be exchanged with all users of P2PIKE on a social network. Additionally, the key-exchange can be triggered manually, but in general, it is executed fully automated.

8.4.2 High Security

Because of the extensive use of the APIs and services of a provider, the security of PIKE and P2PIKE depends on the security of the service provider. The service provider needs to implement the resource sharing in such a way that resources which are shared with a limited number of users are properly secured. The resources should not be accessible for any other users than the ones that are specified by the event creator. Many service providers (e.g., Facebook and Google Calendar) support this type of resource sharing. In these cases, PIKE or P2PIKE do not lower the security provided by the service providers, i.e., the security level is as high as the security level of the used service provider.

Of course, one possible attacker that could tamper the key-exchange is the service provider (e.g., Facebook) itself. When using PIKE, all exchanged keys are stored in the service provider's database, it would be easy to retrieve them from there. When P2PIKE is used, the performed key-exchange can only be intercepted by the service provider before the execution of Step

2 (see Figure 6.5). Here, an active man-in-the-middle attack must be performed by the service provider to be able to decrypt messages during the face-to-face collaboration. Nevertheless, the service provider itself is usually not physically present during the face-to-face collaboration. As a result, it cannot use the exchanged key(s) of PIKE and P2PIKE since the interaction triggered by the devices is not spread through the Internet or any other publicly accessible network. Additionally, a P2PIKE interaction will fail, if a man-in-the-middle attack tampered with the exchanged keys and the man-in-the-middle is not present.

To further mitigate this attack, e.g., if a service provider also deploys hotspots or similar devices so that it might be possible to be physically present during the interaction, service providers can be combined. The trigger condition resource is then distributed to several service providers, all of which must be supported by all participants and the initiator. For enhanced security, the exchanged shared key on the service is different, if the service provider differs. The combination (e.g., XOR) of the exchanged shared keys from all the service providers will then be used by the participants. As a result, one service provider cannot overhear the face-to-face collaboration, because it only knows parts of the key. The cooperation of all involved service providers is then necessary to retrieve the whole key.

Possible attacks that do not involve the service provider as an attacker are attacks from devices that take part in the collaboration (i.e., have received the key for secure communication) or attacks from devices that do not possess the exchanged key, but are just in the vicinity of the interacting partners. For the latter devices, it is not possible to attack the interaction as long as the communication is always encrypted, using a secure encryption protocol (e.g., AES). Any kind of attack is then not based on the security of PIKE, but on the security of the mechanism that is used for encryption.

Additionally, the user-level keys can be used to establish an encrypted private communication channel between two users in the collaboration group established by PIKE (e.g., to remove threats from malicious users or devices). If one of the users that wants to open a private channel to another user is the initiator, the user-level key can be used directly. If two participants want to open a private channel, either the initiator's device can be used as a trusted third party that verifies the authentication of the other users or a key that was exchanged by P2PIKE can be used. The exchange of a shared peer-to-peer key will then enable the devices to communicate with each other using encryption, excluding a malicious participant.

If the initiator of a face-to-face collaboration group is malicious, the whole communication is compromised. From the participant's view, this can only be avoided by not taking part at the face-to-face collaboration at all. In the end, this results in ignoring trigger resources coming from malicious devices or users, i.e., not starting a face-to-face collaboration with malicious initiators. PIKE will not protect the participants' communication, if the initiator of the key-exchange is malicious.

8.4.3 Low Latency

Using two Samsung Galaxy Nexus (2x1.2 GHz ARM CPU, 1 GB RAM) mobile phones that were connected to the Internet via WiFi, we measured the latency of our approach. The mobile phones were running Android OS version 4.1.1. To perform the measurements, we were using the prototypical implementations presented in Section 6.3. All values represent the average of 100 measurements performed by one smartphone.

The minimum latency of the overall approach depends on the synchronization interval t. A typical value for t is 60 minutes, i.e., the mobile application checks the service every hour. Depending on the pervasive application, it can be enough to check for key-exchange requests only once a day. To allow spontaneous meetings, more regular checks are required, resulting in a lower value of t. For choosing the optimal value of t, knowing the performance of PIKE and P2PIKE is an essential factor, we therefore now describe the performance of PIKE and P2PIKE.

PIKE

As depicted in Figure 8.9 and 8.10, there are two possible scenarios: after the creation of the shared trigger, it is either picked up by the initiator's device (Figure 8.9) or by a participant's device (Figure 8.10) after a maximum time of t. For the former, the initiator picks up the shared trigger and adds the shared key to the trigger. It cannot retrieve the user-level keys, since they are not yet available. It then waits for the next synchronization interval. In the meantime, the participants synchronize the trigger resource, retrieve the shared key and attach their individual user-level keys to the trigger. Fulfilling this combined step, they have finished the PIKE message exchange and do not need to synchronize this trigger again. After the synchronization interval, the initiator synchronizes the trigger resource, now retrieving all user-level keys. Since the first pick-up time is not higher than t and the second wait time is exactly t, the PIKE message exchange is finished after a maximum time of $2t$. Similar to that, for the latter, the total time to execute PIKE also results in $2t$.

Depending on the used service, this can be further improved by retrieving the *created_time* (if existing) of the shared trigger. The initiator can then retrieve the *created_time* and reschedule the synchronization interval such that the next PIKE synchronization takes place at the time *created_time*+t. Since between the *created_time* and *created_time*+t all participants will have submitted their user-level keys, the initiator is able to retrieve all user-level keys (and finish the PIKE message flow) after a time of only t.

Regarding our implementations, the actual message flows are similar to the logical protocol flow presented in Figure 6.2. The numbers of messages per step in the implementations differ from that, because one logical step might include several API calls. Using our implementation based on Google Calendar, we find that for the initiator, the minimum number of messages (and Google API calls) is 3 (leaving out Step 1); for a participant it is always 3. We also measured the average time that is needed to perform the PIKE protocol flow (σ depicts the standard deviation). We assume that the user creates the event using Google Calendar (either using a mobile phone or the web-interface) manually (i.e., performed Step 1). Steps 2 and 3 take 535ms ($\sigma = 43$ms), and since the initiator needs to perform Step 5 (255ms ($\sigma = 59$ms) with 2 participants) as well, this gives a total number of 790ms ($\sigma = 73$ms) for the API calls. Each participant needs to execute Steps 2 and 4 which takes 583ms ($\sigma = 170$ms). As a result, we see that the prototypical implementation of PIKE with Google Calendar exhibits a latency of less than a second. Depending on t, also spontaneous meetings can be supported. However, a typical value for t like 60 minutes constrains this to meetings known two hours in advance.

In Facebook, the number of messages changes, because the initiator has to retrieve the user-level keys from each participant's wall. Also, the Facebook Graph API does not give as much detailed information on the events as the Google Calendar API with only one API call. The minimum number of messages (and API calls) for the event initiator is therefore $4 + (n - 1)$ (also performing Steps 2, 3 and 5, with n being the number of participants), while the number for each participant is still 4 (performing Steps 2 and 4). Using the Facebook batch API, n increases only every 50 participants. As discussed before, we assume that the user creates the event from within Facebook (Step 1). The average time necessary to perform the API calls for Steps 2 and 3 is 2193ms ($\sigma = 394$ms). Since on Facebook, Step 5 depends heavily on the number of participants, it is discussed in Section 8.4.4. The participants themselves need to perform Steps 2 and 4, this takes 3067ms ($\sigma = 354$ms). We conclude that the Facebook API has a higher latency, but is still within reasonable limits, with a latency of less than 30 seconds for 200 participants.

8 Evaluation

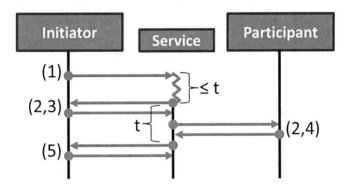

Figure 8.9: Time Needed to Perform PIKE, with Synchronization Interval t (Initiator Before Participant)

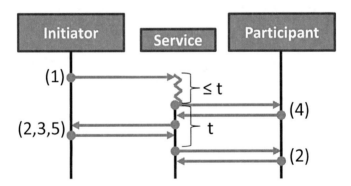

Figure 8.10: Time Needed to Perform PIKE, with Synchronization Interval t (Participant Before Initiator)

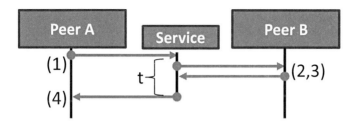

Figure 8.11: Time Needed to Perform P2PIKE

P2PIKE

In contrast to PIKE, P2PIKE executes all steps automatically, including the initial first step. As can be seen in Figure 8.11, P2PIKE needs a time of t to perform the key-exchange with another peer (assuming that their synchronization interval is not completely time-synchronized). At first, Peer A creates a resource and executes the first step of the key-exchange and waits then the time of t before synchronizing the resource again. During that time, Peer B retrieves the resource and executes Step 2 of the key-exchange. Peer B now already has computed the shared secret key. Then Peer A accesses the resource, receives the public key attached by Peer B during the second step of the key-exchange and computes the shared secret key. The total time for the execution of P2PIKE is therefore t.

The measurements of our prototypical implementation are based on 100 Facebook test users and show that Peer A (the initiating peer) needs 3823ms for the execution of Steps 1 and 4 (1378ms ($\sigma = 531$ms) + 2445ms ($\sigma = 430$ms)), i.e., the two API calls. Similarly, Peer B only needs 2336ms ($\sigma = 185$ms) for the execution of Steps 2 and 3. All measurements include the execution time for an ECDH key-exchange (160 bit) to obtain a common key. We conclude that the prototypical implementation of P2PIKE exhibits a low latency.

8.4.4 Scalability

The execution time of P2PIKE depends on the latency of the protocol execution. Since each execution of the P2PIKE protocol flow will create one shared key between two peers, the costs (in time and resources) increase quadratically with the group size. From the point of view of one peer, the costs increase linearly with each newly discovered peer (i.e., +4 seconds/peer,

+1 key/peer, see Section 8.4.3 for more detailed information). Nevertheless, from the point of view of the server (e.g., Facebook), a new peer will use up resources quadratically which could limit its scalability. In our tests, Facebook is easily capable of executing P2PIKE with a group of 100 peers.

For PIKE, scalability depends on the used service. If PIKE is used with Google Calendar, an event contains all information, including user-level keys (as comments). A single API call returns the necessary information. The message's length increases slightly with each participant since a comment is added. Nevertheless, this results in high scalability.

Using Facebook, the number of requests from the event initiator to the service depends heavily on the number of participants. Therefore, we measured PIKE with an increasing number of participants, using single requests (Figure 8.12, showing a clear linear increase, 100 measurements per point, error bars show the standard deviation ($\pm\sigma$)) or batch requests (Figure 8.13, 10 measurements per point, error bars show $\pm\sigma$). Batch requests bundle 50 requests (i.e., one for each participant) in one. Both measurements indicate a linear increase from 1765ms (1 participant) to 7526ms (15 participants) for the single requests and from 1935ms (10 participants) to 21453ms (200 participants) using batch requests. Although the implementation based on Facebook is slower, it still achieves a high scalability using batch requests. In summary, PIKE reaches the scalability goal of supporting a few hundred participants.

8.4.5 Qualitative Evaluation

PIKE is not based on a dedicated central server, but uses existing third-party infrastructure (i.e., online services) to establish shared and user-level keys. As can be seen in the last column of Table 8.6, it therefore suits well the requirements that were derived in Chapter 3. PIKE also does not have any constraints on the number of devices, also supports higher numbers, and is able to create group and user-level keys in a completely automated fashion relying on the friend relationship of online collaboration services. As shown, it is scalable to a high number of users and devices. Also, no Internet connectivity is required at the time the interaction takes place and the secure key is available to all communication partners. As a result, PIKE does not need a third party for account verification during the interaction, but uses a third-party service directly to exchange a shared key beforehand. Summarized, PIKE fulfills our requirements for a secure key-exchange and is an ideal mechanism for the exchange of keys between different users and devices in pervasive environments.

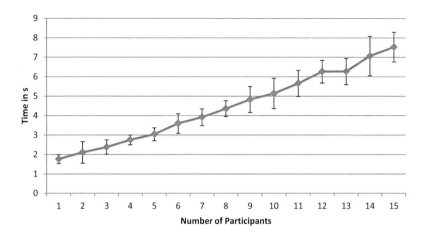

Figure 8.12: Retrieving User-level Keys One-by-one from Facebook

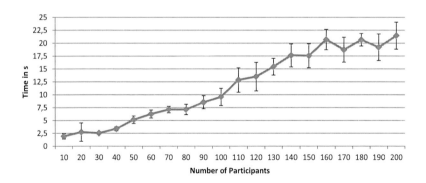

Figure 8.13: Retrieving User-level Keys in a Batch from Facebook

Requirements	Context	Role Assignment	Fulfilled
Peer-to-Peer Infrastructure		Yes	
Decentralized	Yes	Yes	
Highly Scalable	Partially	Yes	
Generic	Yes	Yes	
Environment Boundaries		Yes	
Configurable		Yes	
Flexible		Yes	
Composable		Yes	
Context Privacy and Security	Yes	Yes	
Generic	Yes	Yes	
Reliable Security	Yes	Yes	
Trust		Yes	
Decentralized	Yes	Yes	
Extensible		Yes	
Secure Key-exchange			Yes
Highly Scalable		Partially	Yes
User-Level Authentication			Yes
Key Availability			Yes
Individual Privacy Policy			
Generic			
Automated			
Low Overhead			

Table 8.6: Secure Key-exchange in Comparison to the Requirements

8.5 Automating Policy Generation

As last contribution to the area of system support for pervasive computing, we now evaluate our approach for the automatic generation of privacy policies. For the evaluation, we concentrate on the four design goals that we introduced in Section 7.2.2 and also evaluate the privacy policy generation framework against the requirements derived in Chapter 3. The four design goals were *genericity*, *extensibility*, *automation* and *low overhead*.

8.5.1 Generic

Our approach for the automatic generation of privacy policies does not constrain the type of context, i.e., it is possible to use it with every type of context. Similarly, the approach does also not constrain the recognizer in any way. A context recognizer could support the recognition of context types from any kind of data. Although context types that cannot be recognized by a recognizer are supported, the generated privacy policy will never include these types of context, since they could not be detected. These kinds of unrecognizable context types can be added to the policy manually by the user, though.

Additionally, the privacy policy generation framework does allow for a context type to have different scopes. Usually, the number of scopes and their meaning must be defined by a context-sharing application and the creator of the affected context type(s) (similar to the context type itself for example by using an ontology). When the scope is also supported by the context recognizer, the generated privacy policy does include the proper scope for a recognized context type. The used context types and scopes can be chosen freely. It is therefore possible to use an arbitrary ontology that defines different context types and scopes like the CoBrA ontology [CFJ03].

8.5.2 Extensible

There are several providers with resources that can be used to derive a privacy policy from them. In our implementation, we were using Facebook status messages and Google Calendar events. Additionally, the framework can be extended with other plug-ins. Each plug-in can use one or more resource types from an online collaboration tool for the policy derivation. Only two kinds of information must be accessible and delivered to the framework: (a) the contents of the resource and (b) the users with whom the resource is shared. Using this information, the framework can execute the context recognizers and create permissions for the context types (if at least one is detected). Additionally, a plug-in can also deliver a list of possible context types that the resource can exhibit. This might speed up the context recognition process since the framework will then concentrate the recognition on a subset of all possible context types.

The framework can be extended easily by plug-ins for other online collaboration tools. Additionally, we argue that the threshold for the creation of such plug-ins is low since the plug-ins only need to extract few information from the online collaboration tools and deliver it to the framework.

8.5.3 Automation

The generation of a privacy policy for context-sharing applications is executed fully automatic. All steps depicted in Figure 7.2 can be performed automatically. Plug-ins for the privacy policy framework only need user interaction when the user authorizes the application. The type of authorization depends on the online collaboration tool, but often involves an OAuth-like [Har12] process. This is a one-time process that is required by all applications that use online collaboration tools and makes sure that the user is aware of the applications that might access her private information. The generation of the privacy policy including the recognition of the context types is executed without any user interaction. When the privacy policy is generated and does not conflict with any existing privacy policy, it could be used by context-sharing applications automatically.

Since context recognizers cannot always reliably detect the right context types and users can choose a wrong sharing setting by mistake, the generated privacy policy should be reviewed by the user. This would introduce a manual step, before the policy is applied and stored. Similarly, if a conflicting policy is detected, the user would need to manually resolve this conflict. The framework can prepare possible solutions, but in the end, the user needs to choose the right one. This manual step at the end of the automatic policy generation is inevitable to ensure that the user really agrees to the generated policy. In our implementation, as can be seen in Figure 7.6, we visualize the generated permissions (which form the privacy policy), helping the user in validating the automatically generated privacy policy. Additionally, we provide the user with information on which sharing behavior triggered this permission. This might, as a side effect, also make the user aware of any errors in her sharing settings at online collaboration tools. Beside this manual step, the privacy policy generation is executed fully automatic.

8.5.4 Low Overhead

The overhead for the automatic generation of a privacy policy depends heavily on the used plug-ins for the online collaboration tools and the context recognizers. If, for example, a plug-in transfers high resolution images and lets the context recognizer perform a complicated image processing task (such as face recognition), the overhead is much higher than when only text is transferred and a relatively simple word processing task is executed by a context recognizer. When complicated processing tasks are executed, the

	Mean	Standard deviation
Facebook Plug-in	868 ms	79.4 ms
Context Recognition (location)	0.60 ms	0.081 ms
Privacy Policy Generation	52 ms	16.4 ms

Table 8.7: Measuring the Privacy Policy Generation

framework can ensure that the generation of the privacy policy is only executed when (a) WiFi is available (to avoid exhausting the data plan) and (b) the smart phone is not used (e.g., at night time) and charging (to avoid interference with normal user smartphone interactions).

To validate that the framework itself does not create a high overhead, we measured the steps shown in Figure 7.2. At first, we measured our implemented Facebook plug-in (retrieving status messages, Step 1 and 2), then our context recognizer (detecting the context type *location* using a word list containing names of more than 26500 cities, Step 3) as well as the complete time, executing the privacy policy generator and the context recognizer (Steps 3 to 5), computing and displaying the generated privacy policy to the user. Our measurement setup consists of one Nexus 5 smartphone (OS: Android 4.4.4, CPU: 4x2.26 GHz, 2 GB RAM) that is using a dedicated 2.4 GHz 802.11n WiFi network (provided by a Netgear WNR3500Lv2 access point). We performed each measurement 100 times and computed the average as well as the standard deviation. The results can be seen in Table 8.7. The total time for Steps 1 to 5 stays well below $1000ms$ ($868ms + 52ms$), with a standard deviation of $\sigma = 95.8ms$ ($79.4ms + 16.4ms$).

As can be seen in Table 8.7, the main latency ($868ms$) is introduced by the online social collaboration tool plug-in (here: Facebook). The execution of the privacy policy generator only takes $52ms$, including the context recognition of $0.60ms$. We therefore argue that our framework implementation introduces only a low overhead.

Regarding the amount of data that is transferred, we use the message that is displayed in Figure 7.7 as a reference for an average status message. Facebook status messages can be longer, but often tend to stay well below the maximum length of a Twitter message (which is 140 characters). As can be seen easily from the API representation shown in Figure 7.8, the sharing settings are often longer than the actual message. The status message

Requirements	Context	Role Assignment	PIKE	Fulfilled
Peer-to-Peer Infrastructure		**Yes**		
Decentralized	Yes	Yes		
Highly Scalable	Partially	Yes		
Generic	Yes	Yes		
Environment Boundaries		**Yes**		
Configurable		Yes		
Flexible		Yes		
Composable		Yes		
Context Privacy and Security	Yes	**Yes**		
Generic	Yes	Yes		
Reliable Security	Yes	Yes		
Trust		**Yes**		
Decentralized	Yes	Yes		
Extensible		Yes		
Secure Key-exchange			**Yes**	
Highly Scalable		Partially	Yes	
User-Level Authentication			Yes	
Key Availability			Yes	
Individual Privacy Policy				**Yes**
Generic				Yes
Automated				Yes
Low Overhead				Yes

Table 8.8: The Privacy Policy Generation Framework in Comparison to the Requirements

presented here uses a data volume of 383 bytes. This results in a very low data volume, even if the user has many recent status messages. The data volume that is consumed by 1000 status messages should therefore lie well below 500 kB.

Although the actual data volume and execution time depends on the used plug-ins and context recognizers, we conclude that the components we implemented in our framework only introduce a low overhead. Compared to a user that manually needs to define several privacy policies for different applications, this low overhead actually results in a high advantage. Nevertheless, it is noteworthy that if a context recognizer needs to perform more complex computations and therefore does not exhibit a low overhead, it should use the framework's ability to execute the privacy policy generation during a time where the user does not use the smartphone, i.e., where the generation does not affect normal usage. This could be the case when the smartphone is charging and/or has WiFi connectivity.

8.5.5 Qualitative Evaluation

The privacy policy generator is a continuation of the idea to use online collaboration tools for pervasive computing applications. As can be seen in the last column of Table 8.8, it also fulfills our requirements for the creation of an individual privacy policy. The framework is generic with regard to the type of context that can be included in the policy and all steps that can be executed automatically are automated. Additionally, it has a low overhead and is able to run on resource-constrained devices such as smartphones. As a further proof of its applicability, the concept has been implemented and can be used directly by pervasive computing applications based on the GAMBAS middleware, as demonstrated in Section 7.4.

8.6 Conclusion

When all our approaches are combined, we fill the gaps that were identified in Chapter 3 and resulted in our general requirements. Table 8.9 shows the summarized requirements. Additionally, it can be seen, which approach fulfills which part of the requirements.

The privacy-preserving *Context Management* is fully decentralized and generic to the type of context that can be shared among devices using the query processor that was implemented and adapted in our first approach. Additionally, it supports decentralized trust, which is suitable for secure peer-to-peer interactions. The *Context Distribution* framework added the secure context handling which also preserves the privacy of our context management framework. It is generic to the type of context that shall be protected and is using reliable, Internet-level security. It also has partial support for decentralized trust.

Because our approach for secure adaptation with *Role Assignment* is based on our mechanisms for secure context management and distribution, the secure role assignment fulfills all requirements that are relevant for context security and privacy. Additionally, the approach has an extensible trust model, is highly scalable and allows to define environment boundaries of pervasive environments or smart spaces in a configurable, flexible and composable way.

Requirements	Fulfilled by
Peer-to-Peer Infrastructure	**Role Assignment**
Decentralized	Context Management & Distribution, Role Assignment
Highly Scalable	Role Assignment
Generic	Context Management & Distribution, Role Assignment
Environment Boundaries	**Role Assignment**
Configurable	Role Assignment
Flexible	Role Assignment
Composable	Role Assignment
Context Privacy and Security	**Context Distribution, Role Assignment**
Generic	Context Distribution, Role Assignment
Reliable Security	Context Distribution, Role Assignment
Trust	**Role Assignment**
Decentralized	Context Management & Distribution, Role Assignment
Extensible	Role Assignment
Secure Key-exchange	**PIKE**
Highly Scalable	PIKE
User-Level Authentication	PIKE
Key Availability	PIKE
Individual Privacy Policy	**Privacy Policy Generation**
Generic	Privacy Policy Generation
Automated	Privacy Policy Generation
Low Overhead	Privacy Policy Generation

Table 8.9: All Approaches in Comparison to the Requirements

The secure key-exchange mechanisms *PIKE* and P2PIKE, fulfill the requirements with regard to our concept of a secure key-exchange that is suitable for the pervasive computing domain. The mechanisms are highly scalable, provide a pervasive computing environment with user-level authentication and exchange a secure key before the interaction takes place. As a result, the key is available to the devices and they do not require any Internet connectivity at the moment the interaction takes place.

Our last framework for automating the *Privacy Policy Generation* also satisfies the requirements. The individual privacy policy that is created by the framework is generic to the type of context, fully automated and has only a low overhead which allows it to be executed on resource-constrained devices.

The evaluation has shown that our approaches which were described in the Chapters 4 to 7 are fulfilling the requirements created in Chapter 3 and provide system support for different areas of security and privacy in pervasive computing environments.

9 Conclusions and Outlook

In this thesis, we have presented new innovative approaches for security and privacy in the pervasive computing domain. We have described how security can be integrated in pervasive middlewares, providing system support, and why security in pervasive computing is crucial when using security critical pervasive applications. At the same time, we have presented several prototypical applications that show that our approaches are feasible and can be used to secure pervasive environments or smart spaces.

The introduction of security in the pervasive computing domain is a requirement to be able to use pervasive applications in security critical scenarios. Additionally, applications that share private (context) information also require the information to be transmitted securely and need to be privacy-aware. During the work described in this thesis it has been shown that existing security mechanisms must be redesigned or adapted to the demands of the pervasive computing domain, especially with regard to resource-constrained devices or mobility.

Our work has shown how security and privacy mechanisms can be integrated into a pervasive middleware, providing pervasive applications with Internet-grade security while keeping the overhead low.

The first mechanism that we presented discussed how a privacy-preserving peer-based context management can be created using RDF triples. Additionally, we described a protocol which allows to use context as a security token for access control. The implementation of these mechanisms on resource-poor devices such as sensors and routers using a pervasive middleware showed that this provides an appropriate foundation for pervasive computing scenarios.

The second mechanism described the next logical step for system support in pervasive computing, the transition from context to roles. The role assignment system allows a pervasive middleware to use other means than locality to define the set of devices it interacts with. The roles are based on rules on context and used as basis for environment adaptations. The adaptations adjust the environment or smart space to the needs of the user and can expand the boundaries of a smart space hierarchically such that inter smart space communications are possible and the integrated islands scenarios can be overcome. Because the adaptation decisions might have security critical implications, we integrated security mechanisms into the role assignment service. Beside providing support for security critical pervasive applications, this also allows to use role-based access control with secure role assignment. At the same time, the security extensions to role assignment have been proven to be light-weight and do not decrease the number of supported devices in comparison to our previous approach.

The third mechanism presented in this thesis describes a secure key-exchange for pervasive environments. The common security protocols use a web of trust (PGP/GPG) or certificate hierarchies (TLS/SSL/S-MIME) to validate the authenticity of users. In the pervasive computing domain, certificate hierarchies can be applied when companies form a pervasive domain and can control the devices that interact in this domain. For peer-to-peer communications, a web of trust is more suitable. Our approach exploits the (web of trust-like) relationships of users of online collaboration tools such as Facebook or Google Calendar and exchanges a key using these tools. The key can then be used in real-world face-to-face meetings to automate the identification of a user's device as well as for secure and authenticated (group) communication. This allows a device to automate the creation of secure communication channels.

The fourth mechanism discusses a different approach for the creation of a privacy policy. Many pervasive context-sharing applications require a policy that describes what kind of data should be shared with whom. This policy is then used by the application to decide if context should be shared with another device or not. Often, this has a high influence on the service quality provided by the pervasive application. Our approach tries to exploit the privacy policies that a user already defined in online collaboration tools. For this, the user's past sharing behavior is analyzed and a policy is suggested that describes this behavior best. This automated creation of a privacy policy can give the user additional information on her sharing behavior. Providing an integrated system, the privacy policy is incorporated into a pervasive middleware and can be shared among different applications.

The implementation of security and privacy in the pervasive computing domain requires the mechanisms to be tailored to this domain to keep its properties like full automation, seamless integration, mobility and heterogeneous device support. The approaches that we described in this thesis fulfill these requirements while accomplishing Internet-level security for the pervasive computing domain, allowing an application to be scalable, secure and privacy-aware.

9.1 Outlook

This thesis has described the first steps on security and privacy in the pervasive computing domain. The realization of security and privacy in the area of pervasive computing as well as in adjacent fields like home automation remains an important research topic. Nowadays, private information is shared between users and services and it seems to be increasingly difficult for a user to keep track of her own data.

With the emerging of new context-sharing applications, the pervasive computing community will increase its efforts in security and privacy mechanisms with a focus on secure communication and privacy-preserving context-sharing.

As a first step, the secure role assignment system could be extended to support supplemental models of trust. Specifically, the integration of a trust system which integrates several trust systems such as a reputation-based system and a conventional certificate trust system could provide more flexibility to trust-based decisions.

To be more flexible with regard to users that want to establish a secure communication channel, different key-exchange mechanisms can be created that may be tailored to the different needs of a user. A common key-exchange model that supports technologies like PIKE, NFC or image recognition would allow a user to easily set up a secure communication channel without the use of a password or a PIN which are often cumbersome to create and share.

With regard to privacy of a user, it seems to be necessary to actually analyze the data that is shared between users using online collaboration tools. By displaying the user her current privacy level this could raise awareness for privacy and could allow the emerging of new, privacy-preserving technologies, e.g., by using pseudonyms and/or secure, peer-to-peer communication. The modeling of the privacy level could be seen as a first step into this direction. Also, making the new privacy-preserving technologies user friendly is an important factor to keep the privacy mechanisms as distraction-free as possible for the users.

Bibliography

[ABC+04]   T. Abdelzaher, B. Blum, Q. Cao, Y. Chen, D. Evans,
             J. George, S. George, L. Gu, T. He, S. Krishnamurthy, L. Luo,
             S. Son, J. Stankovic, R. Stoleru, and A. Wood. Enviro-
             track: Towards an environmental computing paradigm for dis-
             tributed sensor networks. In *ICDCS '04: 24th International
             Conference on Distributed Computing Systems*, pages 582–589,
             Washington, DC, USA, 2004. IEEE Computer Society.

[ACC04]   Jalal Al-Muhtadi, Shiva Chetan, and Roy Campbell. Super
             spaces: A middleware for large-scale pervasive computing en-
             vironment perware '04. In *IEEE International Workshop on
             Pervasive Computing and Communications*, pages 198–202,
             2004.

[AHIM13a]   Wolfgang Apolinarski, Marcus Handte, Muhammad Umer
             Iqbal, and Pedro José Marrón. PIggy-backed Key Exchange
             using Online Services (PIKE). In *Pervasive Computing and
             Communications Workshops (PERCOM Workshops), 2013
             IEEE International Conference on*, March 2013.

[AHIM13b]   Wolfgang Apolinarski, Marcus Handte, Umer Iqbal, and Pe-
             dro José Marrón. PIKE: Enabling secure interaction with pig-
             gybacked key-exchange. In *Pervasive Computing and Com-
             munications (PerCom), 2013 IEEE International Conference
             on*, pages 94–102, 2013.

[AHIM14]   Wolfgang Apolinarski, Marcus Handte, Muhammad Umer
             Iqbal, and Pedro José Marrón. Secure interaction with pig-
             gybacked key-exchange. *Pervasive and Mobile Computing*, 10,
             Part A(0), 2014. Selected Papers from the Eleventh Annual
             IEEE Int. Conf. on Pervasive Computing and Communications
             (PerCom 2013).

[AHM10]   Wolfgang Apolinarski, Marcus Handte, and Pedro José
             Marrón. A secure context distribution framework for peer-
             based pervasive systems. In *PerWare Workshop at the 8th*

Annual IEEE International Conference on Pervasive Computing and Communications, March 2010.

[AHM11]   Wolfgang Apolinarski, Marcus Handte, and Pedro José Marrón. Supporting environment configuration with generic role assignment. In *Intelligent Environments (IE), 2011 7th International Conference on*, pages 1 –8, July 2011.

[AHM12]   Wolfgang Apolinarski, Marcus Handte, and Pedro José Marrón. An approach for secure role assignment. In *Intelligent Environments (IE), 2012 8th International Conference on*, June 2012.

[AHM15]   Wolfgang Apolinarski, Marcus Handte, and Pedro José Marrón. Automating the generation of privacy policies for context-sharing applications. In *Intelligent Environments (IE), 2015 11th International Conference on*, July 2015.

[AHPM11] Wolfgang Apolinarski, Marcus Handte, Danh Le Phuoc, and Pedro José Marrón. A peer-based approach to privacy-preserving context management. In *Modeling and Using Context - 7th International and Interdisciplinary Conference, CONTEXT 2011, Karlsruhe, Germany, September 26-30, 2011. Proceedings*, pages 18–25, 2011.

[AIP14]   Wolfgang Apolinarski, Umer Iqbal, and Josiane Xavier Parreira. The GAMBAS middleware and SDK for smart city applications. In *Pervasive Computing and Communications Workshops (PerCity 2014, PERCOM Workshops), 2014 IEEE International Conference on*, March 2014.

[AKM07]   Erwin Aitenbichler, Jussi Kangasharju, and Max Mühlhäuser. Mundocore: A light-weight infrastructure for pervasive computing. *Pervasive and Mobile Computing*, 3(4):332–361, August 2007.

[Ali11]   Mohannad Ali. Gathering and matching of user information derived from social networks. Bachelor's thesis, Universität Duisburg-Essen, March 2011.

[AMHCM06] Jalal Al-Muhtadi, Raquel Hill, Roy Campbell, and M. Dennis Mickunas. Context and location-aware encryption for pervasive computing environments. In *Pervasive Computing and Communications Workshops, 2006. PerCom Workshops 2006. Fourth Annual IEEE International Conference on*, pages 6 pp.–289, March 2006.

[Apa]   Apache Jena project team. Jena, a java framework for building
              semantic web applications, http://jena.apache.org.

[Apo15]   Wolfgang Apolinarski. Establishing secure intelligent environ-
              ments. In *Workshop Proceedings of the 11th International
              Conference on Intelligent Environments, Prague, Czech Re-
              public, July 15-17, 2015*, pages 43–45, 2015.

[BCQ⁺07]   Cristiana Bolchini, Carlo Curino, Elisa Quintarelli, Fabio A.
              Schreiber, and Letizia Tanca. A data-oriented survey of con-
              text models. *SIGMOD Record*, 36(4):19–26, December 2007.

[BDR07]   Matthias Baldauf, Schahram Dustdar, and Florian Rosenberg.
              A survey on context-aware systems. *International Journal of
              Ad Hoc and Ubiquitous Computing*, 2:263–277, June 2007.

[Bec04]   Christian Becker. *System-support for context-aware comput-
              ing*. Habilitationsschrift, Fakultät Informatik, Elektrotechnik
              und Informationstechnik, Universität Stuttgart, June 2004.

[BHSR04]   Christian Becker, Marcus Handte, Gregor Schiele, and Kurt
              Rothermel. PCOM - a component system for pervasive com-
              puting. In *2nd IEEE International Conference on Perva-
              sive Computing and Communications (PerCom'04)*, page 67,
              Washington, DC, USA, 2004. IEEE Computer Society.

[BKK⁺09]   Joppe W. Bos, Marcelo E. Kaihara, Thorsten Kleinjung, Ar-
              jen K. Lenstra, and Peter L. Montgomery. On the security of
              1024-bit RSA and 160-bit elliptic curve cryptography. *IACR
              Cryptology ePrint Archive*, 2009:389, 2009.

[Blu07]   Bluetooth SIG.   Specification of the bluetooth system,
              core version 2.1 + EDR, https://www.bluetooth.org/en-
              us/specification/adopted-specifications, July 2007.

[BMK⁺00]   Barry Brumitt, Brian Meyers, John Krumm, Amanda Kern,
              and Steven A. Shafer. Easyliving: Technologies for intelligent
              environments. In *Proceedings of the 2nd international sympo-
              sium on Handheld and Ubiquitous Computing*, HUC '00, pages
              12–29, London, UK, UK, 2000. Springer-Verlag.

[BSGR03]   Christian Becker, Gregor Schiele, Holger Gubbels, and Kurt
              Rothermel. BASE - A micro-broker-based middleware for per-
              vasive computing. In *Proceedings of the First IEEE Interna-
              tional Conference on Pervasive Computing and Communica-*

tions (PerCom'03), March 23-26, 2003, Fort Worth, Texas, USA, pages 443–451, March 2003.

[BSHL07] Daniel Bichler, Guido Stromberg, Mario Huemer, and Manuel Löw. Key generation based on acceleration data of shaking processes. In *Proceedings of the 9th International Conference on Ubiquitous Computing (Innsbruck, Austria)*, volume 4717 of *UbiComp '07*, pages 304–317. Springer, September 2007.

[CC11] Yohan Chon and Hojung Cha. Lifemap: A smartphone-based context provider for location-based services. *Pervasive Computing, IEEE*, 10(2):58–67, April 2011.

[CCK+08] Chia-Hsin Owen Chen, Chung-Wei Chen, Cynthia Kuo, Yan-Hao Lai, Jonathan M. McCune, Ahren Studer, Adrian Perrig, Bo-Yin Yang, and Tzong-Chen Wu. Gangs: gather, authenticate 'n group securely. In *Proceedings of the 14th Annual International Conference on Mobile Computing and Networking, MOBICOM 2008, San Francisco, California, USA, September 14-19, 2008*, pages 92–103, 2008.

[CFJ03] Harry Chen, Tim Finin, and Anupam Joshi. An ontology for context-aware pervasive computing environments. *Special Issue on Ontologies for Distributed Systems, Knowledge Engineering Review*, 18(3):197–207, September 2003.

[CFJ04] Harry Chen, Tim Finin, and Anupam Joshi. Semantic web in the context broker architecture. In *2nd IEEE Intl. Conference on Pervasive Comp. and Comm.*, page 277, 2004.

[CGS+03] Vinny Cahill, Elizabeth Gray, Jean-Marc Seigneur, Christian Damsgaard Jensen, Yong Chen, Brian Shand, Nathan Dimmock, Andrew Twigg, Jean Bacon, Colin English, Waleed Wagealla, Sotirios Terzis, Paddy Nixon, Giovanna Di Marzo Serugendo, Ciarán Bryce, Marco Carbone, Karl Krukow, and Mogens Nielsen. Using trust for secure collaboration in uncertain environments. *IEEE Pervasive Computing*, 2(3):52–61, 2003.

[CPFJ04] Harry Chen, Filip Perich, Tim Finin, and Anupam Joshi. Soupa: Standard ontology for ubiquitous and pervasive applications. *Mobile and Ubiquitous Systems, Annual International Conference on*, pages 258–267, 2004.

[CSF⁺08]   D. Cooper, S. Santesson, S. Farrell, S. Boeyen, R. Housley, and
           W. Polk. Internet X.509 Public Key Infrastructure Certificate
           and Certificate Revocation List (CRL) Profile. RFC 5280,
           May 2008.

[DA99]   Anind K. Dey and Gregory D. Abowd. Towards a better un-
           derstanding of context and context-awareness. Technical re-
           port GIT-GVU-99-22, College of Computing, Georgia Insti-
           tute of Technology, Atlanta, GA, USA, 1999.

[Dan09]   George Danezis. Inferring privacy policies for social network-
           ing services. In *Proceedings of the 2nd ACM Workshop on
           Security and Artificial Intelligence, AISec 2009, Chicago, Illi-
           nois, USA, November 9, 2009*, AISec '09, pages 5–10, New
           York, NY, USA, 2009. ACM.

[DAS01]   Anind K. Dey, Gregory D. Abowd, and Daniel Salber. A con-
           ceptual framework and a toolkit for supporting the rapid pro-
           totyping of context-aware applications. *Human-Computer In-
           teraction*, 16(2-4):97–166, December 2001.

[ETR]   ETRA Investigación y Desarrollo, S.A. ETRA I+D. Valencia,
           Spain, http://www.grupoetra.com.

[FC04]   Patrick Fahy and Siobhan Clarke. Cass - a middleware for
           mobile context-aware applications. In *Workshop on Context
           Awareness, MobiSys*, 2004.

[FHMM10]   Lishoy Francis, Gerhard Hancke, Keith Mayes, and Konstanti-
           nos Markantonakis. Practical NFC peer-to-peer relay attack
           using mobile phones. In *Radio Frequency Identification: Secu-
           rity and Privacy Issues - 6th International Workshop, RFID-
           Sec 2010, Istanbul, Turkey, June 8-9, 2010, Revised Selected
           Papers*, RFIDSec'10, pages 35–49, 2010.

[FL10]   Lujun Fang and Kristen LeFevre. Privacy wizards for social
           networking sites. In *Proceedings of the 19th International Con-
           ference on World Wide Web*, WWW '10, pages 351–360, New
           York, NY, USA, 2010. ACM.

[FR05]   Christian Frank and Kay Römer. Algorithms for generic role
           assignment in wireless sensor networks. In *Proceedings of the
           3rd International Conference on Embedded Networked Sensor
           Systems, SenSys 2005, San Diego, California, USA, November
           2-4, 2005*, pages 230–242, NY, USA, 2005. ACM.

[Fro]   FrontEndART Software Ltd. FrontEndART. Szeged, Hungary,
            https://frontendart.com.

[GAM12]   GAMBAS Consortium.   GAMBAS: Generic Adaptive
            Middleware for Behavior-driven Autonomous Services,
            http://www.gambas-ict.eu, 2012.

[GM]   Alberto Zambrano Galbis and Manuel Serrano Matoses.
            ETRA I+D PECES Traffic Application. Valencia, Spain,
            http://www.grupoetra.com.

[GPZ05]   Tao Gu, Hung Keng Pung, and Da Qing Zhang. A service-
            oriented middleware for building context-aware services. *Jour-
            nal Networt and Computer Applications*, 28(1):1–18, January
            2005.

[GSS02]   David Garlan, Daniel P. Siewiorek, and Peter Steenkiste.
            Project Aura: toward distraction-free pervasive computing.
            IEEE Pervasive Computing, 1:22–31, 2002.

[GWPZ04]   Tao Gu, Xiao Hang Wang, Hung Keng Pung, and Da Qing
            Zhang. An ontology-based context model in intelligent envi-
            ronments. In *Communication Networks and Distributed Sys-
            tems Modeling and Simulation Conference*, pages 270–275,
            2004.

[Har12]   Dick Hardt. The OAuth 2.0 authorization framework, draft-
            ietf-oauth-v2-31, July 2012.

[HB06]   Ernst Haselsteiner and Klemens Breitfuß. Security in near
            field communication (NFC). In *Workshop on RFID Security*,
            2006.

[HBS03]   Marcus Handte, Christian Becker, and Gregor Schiele. Expe-
            riences - extensibility and minimalism in BASE. In *Workshop
            System Support for Ubiquitous Computing (UbiSys) at Ubi-
            comp*, 2003.

[HH07]   Olaf Hartig and Ralf Heese. The sparql query graph model
            for query optimization. In *Proceedings of the 4th European
            conference on The Semantic Web: Research and Applications*,
            ESWC '07, pages 564–578, Berlin, Heidelberg, 2007. Springer-
            Verlag.

[HHM09]   Muhammad Haroon, Marcus Handte, and Pedro José Marrón. Generic role assignment: A uniform middleware abstraction for configuration of pervasive systems. *PerWare Workshop at the 7th Annual IEEE International Conference on Pervasive Computing and Communications*, 2009.

[HIA$^+$10]   Marcus Handte, Umer Iqbal, Wolfgang Apolinarski, Stephan Wagner, and Pedro José Marrón. The NARF architecture for generic personal context recognition. In *Sensor Networks, Ubiquitous, and Trustworthy Computing (SUTC), 2010 IEEE International Conference on*, pages 123–130, June 2010.

[HIMB05]   Karen Henricksen, Jadwiga Indulska, Ted McFadden, and Sasitharan Balasubramaniam. Middleware for distributed context-aware systems. In *On the Move to Meaningful Internet Systems 2005: CoopIS, DOA, and ODBASE, OTM Confederated International Conferences CoopIS, DOA, and ODBASE 2005, Agia Napa, Cyprus, October 31 - November 4, 2005, Proceedings, Part I*, pages 846–863, 2005.

[HL04]   Jason I. Hong and James A. Landay. An architecture for privacy-sensitive ubiquitous computing. In *Proceedings of the Second International Conference on Mobile Systems, Applications, and Services, MobiSys 2004, Hyatt Harborside, Boston, Massachusetts, USA, June 6-9, 2004*, pages 177–189, 2004.

[HL10]   Eran Hammer-Lahav. The OAuth 1.0 protocol, April 2010.

[HMS$^+$01]   Lars Erik Holmquist, Friedemann Mattern, Bernt Schiele, Petteri Alahuhta, Michael Beigl, and Hans Gellersen. Smart-its friends: A technique for users to easily establish connections between smart artefacts. In *Ubicomp 2001: Proceedings of the 3rd international conference on Ubiquitous Computing, Atlanta, Georgia, USA*, pages 116–122. Springer-Verlag, 2001.

[HSP$^+$03]   Thomas Hofer, Wieland Schwinger, Mario Pichler, Gerhard Leonhartsberger, Josef Altmann, and Werner Retschitzegger. Context-awareness on mobile devices - the hydrogen approach. In *36th Hawaii International Conference on System Sciences*, HICSS '03, 2003.

[HWMI05]   Karen Henricksen, Ryan Wishart, Ted McFadden, and Jadwiga Indulska. Extending context models for privacy in pervasive computing environments. In *3rd IEEE Conference on*

Pervasive Computing and Communications Workshops (PerCom 2005 Workshops), 8-12 March 2005, Kauai Island, HI, USA, pages 20–24, March 2005.

[HWS⁺10] Marcus Handte, Stephan Wagner, Gregor Schiele, Christian Becker, and Pedro José Marrón. The BASE plug-in architecture - composable communication support for pervasive systems. In *7th ACM International Conference on Pervasive Services*, July 2010.

[HYS05] Dan Hong, Mingxuan Yuan, and Vincent Y. Shen. Dynamic privacy management: A plug-in service for the middleware in pervasive computing. In *Proceedings of the 7th International Conference on Human Computer Interaction with Mobile Devices & Services*, MobileHCI '05, pages 1–8, New York, NY, USA, 2005. ACM.

[IFW⁺13] Muhammad Umer Iqbal, Ngewi Fet, Stephan Wagner, Marcus Handte, and Pedro José Marrón. Living++: A platform for assisted living applications. In *Proceedings of the 2013 ACM Conference on Pervasive and Ubiquitous Computing Adjunct Publication*, UbiComp '13 Adjunct, pages 853–860, New York, NY, USA, 2013. ACM.

[IHW⁺12] Muhammad Umer Iqbal, Marcus Handte, Stephan Wagner, Wolfgang Apolinarski, and Pedro José Marrón. Enabling energy-efficient context recognition with configuration folding. In *2012 IEEE International Conference on Pervasive Computing and Communications, Lugano, Switzerland, March 19-23, 2012*, pages 198–205, march 2012.

[INPS03] Luca Iocchi, Daniele Nardi, Maurizio Piaggio, and Antonio Sgorbissa. Distributed coordination in heterogeneous multi-robot systems. *Autonomous Robots*, 15(2):155–168, 2003.

[KBC97] H. Krawczyk, M. Bellare, and R. Canetti. HMAC: Keyed-Hashing for Message Authentication. RFC 2104, February 1997.

[KFJ01] Lalana Kagal, Tim Finin, and Anupam Joshi. Trust-based security in pervasive computing environments. *IEEE Computer*, 34(12):154–157, December 2001.

[KFJ03] Lalana Kagal, Tim Finin, and Anupam Joshi. A policy language for a pervasive computing environment. In *Proceedings of the 4th IEEE International Workshop on Policies for*

Distributed Systems and Networks, POLICY '03, Washington, DC, USA, 2003. IEEE Computer Society.

[KJ07]   Sanem Kabadayi and Christine Julien. A local data abstraction and communication paradigm for pervasive computing. In *5th IEEE International Conference on Pervasive Computing and Communications (PerCom'07)*, pages 57–68, 2007.

[KLJ⁺08]   Seungwoo Kang, Jinwon Lee, Hyukjae Jang, Hyonik Lee, Youngki Lee, Souneil Park, Taiwoo Park, and Junehwa Song. SeeMon: scalable and energy-efficient context monitoring framework for sensor-rich mobile environments. In *Proceedings of the 6th International Conference on Mobile Systems, Applications, and Services (MobiSys 2008), Breckenridge, CO, USA, June 17-20, 2008*, 2008.

[KM03]   Panu Korpipää and Jani Mäntyjärvi. An ontology for mobile device sensor-based context awareness. In *4th international and interdisciplinary conference on modeling and using context*, pages 451–458, 2003.

[KNS05]   Karl Krukow, Mogens Nielsen, and Vladimiro Sassone. A framework for concrete reputation-systems with applications to history-based access control. In *Proceedings of the 12th ACM Conference on Computer and Communications Security, CCS 2005, Alexandria, VA, USA, November 7-11, 2005*, CCS '05, pages 260–269, New York, NY, USA, 2005. ACM.

[KUP⁺02]   Lalana Kagal, Jeffrey Undercoffer, Filip Perich, Anupam Joshi, and Tim Finin. A security architecture based on trust management for pervasive computing systems. In *Grace Hopper Celebration of Women in Computing*, October 2002.

[LBP⁺11]   Hong Lu, A. J. Bernheim Brush, Bodhi Priyantha, Amy K. Karlson, and Jie Liu. Speakersense: Energy efficient unobtrusive speaker identification on mobile phones. In *Proceedings of the 9th International Conference on Pervasive Computing*, Pervasive'11, pages 188–205, Berlin, Heidelberg, 2011. Springer-Verlag.

[LKPW09]   Brent Lagesse, Mohan Kumar, Justin Mazzola Paluska, and Matthew Wright. DTT: a distributed trust toolkit for pervasive systems. In *Pervasive Computing and Communications, 2009. PerCom 2009. IEEE International Conference on*, pages 1–8, 2009.

[LSH+09]   Yue-Hsun Lin, Ahren Studer, Hsu-Chin Hsiao, Jonathan M. Mccune, King-Hang Wang, Maxwell Krohn, Phen-Lan Lin, Adrian Perrig, Hung-Min Sun, and Bo-Yin Yang. Spate: small-group pki-less authenticated trust establishment. In *Proceedings of the 7th international conference on Mobile systems, applications, and services*, MobiSys '09, pages 1–14, New York, NY, USA, 2009. ACM.

[May07]   Rene Mayrhofer. The candidate key protocol for generating secret shared keys from similar sensor data streams. In *Security and Privacy in Ad-hoc and Sensor Networks*, volume 4572 of *Lecture Notes in Computer Science*, pages 1–15. Springer Berlin Heidelberg, 2007.

[MG07]   Rene Mayrhofer and Hans Gellersen. Shake well before use: Authentication based on accelerometer data. In *Pervasive Computing*, volume 4480 of *Lecture Notes in Computer Science*, pages 144–161. Springer Berlin Heidelberg, 2007.

[MLF+08]   Emiliano Miluzzo, Nicholas D. Lane, Kristóf Fodor, Ronald Peterson, Hong Lu, Mirco Musolesi, Shane B. Eisenman, Xiao Zheng, and Andrew T. Campbell. Sensing meets mobile social networks: The design, implementation and evaluation of the cenceme application. In *Proceedings of the 6th ACM Conference on Embedded Network Sensor Systems*, SenSys '08, pages 337–350, New York, NY, USA, 2008. ACM.

[MLKS08]   Gerald Madlmayr, Josef Langer, Christian Kantner, and Josef Scharinger. NFC devices: Security and privacy. In *Proceedings of the The Third International Conference on Availability, Reliability and Security, ARES 2008, March 4-7, 2008, Technical University of Catalonia, Barcelona , Spain*, pages 642–647, March 2008.

[MMV+11]   Suhas Mathur, Robert Miller, Alexander Varshavsky, Wade Trappe, and Narayan Mandayam. ProxiMate: proximity-based secure pairing using ambient wireless signals. In *Proceedings of the 9th International Conference on Mobile Systems, Applications, and Services (MobiSys 2011), Bethesda, MD, USA, June 28 - July 01, 2011*, MobiSys '11, pages 211–224, New York, NY, USA, 2011. ACM.

[MP06]   Luca Mottola and Gian Pietro Picco. Using logical neighborhoods to enable scoping in wireless sensor networks. In *MDS*

'06: 3rd international Middleware doctoral symposium, page 6, NY, USA, 2006. ACM.

[MPR05]   Jonathan M. McCune, Adrian Perrig, and Michael K. Reiter. Seeing-is-believing: Using camera phones for human-verifiable authentication. In *2005 IEEE Symposium on Security and Privacy (S&P 2005), 8-11 May 2005, Oakland, CA, USA*, pages 110–124, 2005.

[MYA⁺05]   Jianhua Ma, Laurence T. Yang, Bernady O. Apduhan, Runhe Huang, Leonard Barolli, Makoto Takizawa, and Timothy K. Shih. A walkthrough from smart spaces to smart hyperspaces towards a smart world with ubiquitous intelligence. In *IC-PADS '05: 11th International Conference on Parallel and Distributed Systems*, pages 370–376, Washington, DC, USA, 2005. IEEE Computer Society.

[NBL⁺10]   Qun Ni, Elisa Bertino, Jorge Lobo, Carolyn Brodie, Clare-Marie Karat, John Karat, and Alberto Trombeta. Privacy-aware role-based access control. *TISSEC ACM Transactions on Information and System Security*, 13(3):24:1–24:31, July 2010.

[NGMW08]   Daniela Nicklas, Matthias Grossmann, Jorge Monguez, and Matthias Wieland. Adding high-level reasoning to efficient low-level context management: A hybrid approach. *IEEE Intl. Conference on Pervasive Computing and Communications*, pages 447–452, 2008.

[NKI03]   Yang Ni, Ulrich Kremer, and Liviu Iftode. Spatial views: Space-aware programming for networks of embedded systems. In *16th International Workshop on Languages and Compilers for Parallel Computing (LCPC 2003*, 2003.

[NW04]   Ryan Newton and Matt Welsh. Region streams: functional macroprogramming for sensor networks. In *Proceedings of the 1st Workshop on Data Management for Sensor Networks, in conjunction with VLDB, DMSN 2004, Toronto, Canada, August 30, 2004*, pages 78–87, NY, USA, 2004.

[Ope07]   OpenID Foundation. OpenID authentication 2.0 - final, http://specs.openid.net/auth/2.0, December 2007.

[PBD⁺14]   Damian Philipp, Patrick Baier, Christoph Dibak, Frank Dürr, Kurt Rothermel, Susanne Becker, Michael Peter, and Dieter

Fritsch. MapGENIE: grammar-enhanced indoor map construction from crowd-sourced data. In *IEEE International Conference on Pervasive Computing and Communications, PerCom 2014, Budapest, Hungary, March 24-28, 2014*, pages 139–147, 2014.

[PEC10]   PECES Consortium. PECES: PErvasive Computing in Embedded Systems, http://www.ict-peces.eu, 2010.

[PJKF03]   Shankar R. Ponnekanti, Brad Johanson, Emre Kiciman, and Armando Fox. Portability, extensibility and robustness in iros. In *PERCOM '03: 1st IEEE International Conference on Pervasive Computing and Communications*, pages 11–19, Washington, DC, USA, 2003. IEEE Computer Society.

[RB]   Zoltan Rak and Vilmos Bilicki. FrontEndART PECES eHealth Application. Szeged, Hungary.

[RB04]   Philip Robinson and Michael Beigl. Trust context spaces: An infrastructure for pervasive security in context-aware environments. In *Security in Pervasive Computing*, volume 2802 of *Lecture Notes in Computer Science*, pages 157–172. Springer Berlin Heidelberg, 2004.

[RB14]   Daniele Riboni and Claudio Bettini. Differentially-private release of check-in data for venue recommendation. In *Pervasive Computing and Communications (PerCom), 2014 IEEE International Conference on*, March 2014.

[RHC+02]   Manuel Román, Christopher Hess, Renato Cerqueira, Anand Ranganathan, Roy H. Campbell, and Klara Nahrstedt. Gaia: a middleware platform for active spaces. *Mobile Computing and Communications Review*, 6(4):65–67, 2002.

[RJH02]   Gruia-Catalin Roman, Christine Julien, and Qingfend Huang. Network abstractions for context-aware mobile computing. In *ICSE '02: 24th International Conference on Software Engineering*, pages 363–373, NY, USA, 2002.

[Rud01]   Larry Rudolph. Project oxygen: Pervasive, human-centric computing - an initial experience. In *CAiSE '01: 13th International Conference on Advanced Information Systems Engineering*, pages 1–12, London, UK, 2001. Springer-Verlag.

[Ser04]   Giovanna Di Marzo Serugendo. Trust as an interaction mechanism for self-organising systems. In *International Conference on Complex Systems (ICCS'04)*, 2004.

[SFH09]   Holger Schmidt, Florian Flerlage, and Franz J. Hauck. A generic context service for ubiquitous environments. In *Seventh Annual IEEE International Conference on Pervasive Computing and Communications - Workshops (PerCom Workshops 2009), 9-13 March 2009, Galveston, TX, USA*, pages 1–6, 2009.

[SHC+12]   Pravin Shankar, Yun-Wu Huang, Paul Castro, Badri Nath, and Liviu Iftode. Crowds replace experts: Building better location-based services using mobile social network interactions. In *2012 IEEE International Conference on Pervasive Computing and Communications, Lugano, Switzerland, March 19-23, 2012*, pages 20–29, 2012.

[SS13]   Dominik Schürmann and Stephan Sigg. Secure communication based on ambient audio. *Mobile Computing, IEEE Transactions on*, 12(2):358–370, 2013.

[SSJ12]   Stephan Sigg, Dominik Schürmann, and Yusheng Ji. Pintext: A framework for secure communication based on context. In *Mobile and Ubiquitous Systems: Computing, Networking, and Services*, volume 104 of *Lecture Notes of the Institute for Computer Sciences, Social Informatics and Telecommunications Engineering*, pages 314–325. Springer Berlin Heidelberg, 2012.

[SVA07]   Jani Suomalainen, Jukka Valkonen, and N. Asokan. Security associations in personal networks: A comparative analysis. In *Security and Privacy in Ad-hoc and Sensor Networks, 4th European Workshop, ESAS 2007, Cambridge, UK, July 2-3, 2007, Proceedings*, pages 43–57, 2007.

[TAJ07]   Hassan Takabi, Morteza Amini, and Rasool Jalili. Trust-based user-role assignment in role-based access control. In *2007 IEEE/ACS International Conference on Computer Systems and Applications (AICCSA 2007), 13-16 May 2007, Amman, Jordan*, pages 807–814, 2007.

[TAK+04]   Anand R. Tripathi, Tanvir Ahmed, Devdatta Kulkarni, Richa Kumar, and Komal Kashiramka. Context-based secure resource access in pervasive computing environments. In *2nd*

IEEE Conference on Pervasive Computing and Communications Workshops (PerCom 2004 Workshops), 14-17 March 2004, Orlando, FL, USA, pages 159–163, March 2004.

[The]   The Legion of the Bouncy Castle. Bouncy Castle Java lightweight cryptography API. http://www.bouncycastle.org, version 1.44, released on the 6th October 2009.

[Toc14]   Eran Toch. Crowdsourcing privacy preferences in context-aware applications. *Personal and Ubiquitous Computing*, 18(1):129–141, 2014.

[TSH10]   Eran Toch, Norman M. Sadeh, and Jason Hong. Generating default privacy policies for online social networks. In *CHI '10 Extended Abstracts on Human Factors in Computing Systems*, CHI EA '10, New York, NY, USA, 2010. ACM.

[VSCY09]   Nitya Vyas, Anna Cinzia Squicciarini, Chih-Cheng Chang, and Danfeng Yao. Towards automatic privacy management in web 2.0 with semantic analysis on annotations. In *The 5th International Conference on Collaborative Computing: Networking, Applications and Worksharing, CollaborateCom 2009, Washington DC, USA, November 11-14, 2009*, pages 1–10, November 2009.

[W3C06]   W3C, P3P Working Group. The Platform for Privacy Preferences 1.1 (P3P1.1) Specification, http://www.w3.org/tr/p3p11/, November 2006.

[Wal02]   Dan S. Wallach. A survey of peer-to-peer security issues. In *Software Security – Theories and Systems, Mext-NSF-JSPS International Symposium, ISSS 2002, Tokyo, Japan, November 8-10, 2002, Revised Papers*, pages 42–57, 2002.

[WDR12]   Marius Wernke, Frank Dürr, and Kurt Rothermel. Pshare: Position sharing for location privacy based on multi-secret sharing. In *Pervasive Computing and Communications (PerCom), 2012 IEEE International Conference on*, pages 153–161, March 2012.

[Wei91]   Mark Weiser. The computer for the 21st century. *Scientific American*, 265(3):94–104, 1991.

[WHZM13]   Stephan Wagner, Marcus Handte, Marco Zuniga, and Pedro José Marrón. Enhancing the performance of indoor localization using multiple steady tags. *Pervasive and Mobile Computing*, 9(3):392–405, June 2013.

[WM04]   Matt Welsh and Geoff Mainland. Programming sensor networks using abstract regions. In *NSDI'04: Proceedings of the 1st conference on Symposium on Networked Systems Design and Implementation*, pages 3–3, Berkeley, CA, USA, 2004.

[Wora]   World Wide Web Consortium. Resource description framework, http://www.w3.org/standards/techs/rdf.

[Worb]   World Wide Web Consortium. SPARQL query language for RDF, http://www.w3.org/tr/rdf-sparql-query/.

[WSBC04]   Kamin Whitehouse, Cory Sharp, Eric Brewer, and David Culler. Hood: a neighborhood abstraction for sensor networks. In *MobiSys '04: 2nd international conference on Mobile systems, applications, and services*, pages 99–110, NY, USA, 2004. ACM.

[WZGP04]   Xiaohang Wang, Daqing Zhang, Tao Gu, and Hung Keng Pung. Ontology based context modeling and reasoning using owl. In *Pervasive Computing and Communications Workshops, 2004. Proceedings of the Second IEEE Annual Conference on*, pages 18–22, 2004.

[YGG+03]   Stephen S. Yau, Sandeep K. S. Gupta, Eep K. S. Gupta, Fariaz Karim, Sheikh I. Ahamed, Yu Wang, and Bin Wang. Smart classroom: Enhancing collaborative learning using pervasive computing technology. In *In ASEE 2003 Annual Conference and Exposition*, pages 13633–13642, 2003.

[ZGW05]   Daqing Zhang, Tao Gu, and Xiaohang Wang. Enabling context-aware smart home with semantic technology. *International Journal of Human-friendly Welfare Robotic Systems*, 6(4):12–20, 2005.